The Teacher's Guide to Oppositional Defiant Disorder

The Teacher's Guide to
OPPOSITIONAL DEFIANT DISORDER

Supporting and Engaging Pupils with Challenging or Disruptive Behaviour in the Classroom

Amelia Bowler

Foreword by Amanda Morin

Jessica Kingsley Publishers
London and Philadelphia

First published in Great Britain in 2022 by Jessica Kingsley Publishers
An imprint of Hodder & Stoughton Ltd
An Hachette Company

4

Copyright © Amelia Bowler 2022
Illustrations copyright © Amelia Bowler 2022

The right of Amelia Bowler to be identified as the Author of the Work has been asserted
by her in accordance with the Copyright, Designs and Patents Act 1988.

Front cover image source: Shutterstock®. The cover image is for illustrative
purposes only, and any person featuring is a model.

A CIP catalogue record for this title is available from the British Library and the Library of Congress

ISBN 978 1 78775 933 6
eISBN 978 1 78775 934 3

Printed and bound by CPI Group (UK) Ltd, Croydon, CR0 4YY

Jessica Kingsley Publishers' policy is to use papers that are natural, renewable and recyclable
products and made from wood grown in sustainable forests. The logging and manufacturing
processes are expected to conform to the environmental regulations of the country of origin.

Jessica Kingsley Publishers
Carmelite House
50 Victoria Embankment
London EC4Y 0DZ

www.jkp.com

Contents

Part IV: Worksheets

Foreword

AMANDA MORIN[1]

Encouraging autonomy and actively building trust aren't likely to be the first strategies that come to mind for engaging with students whose behavior challenges your sense of self-efficacy and your ability to keep your classroom "under control." In fact, many teachers, when faced with students whom they feel challenged and disrespected by, are tempted to double down on techniques that reestablish their authority and attempt to ensure students know that the teacher is in charge.

Yet, students already know who is "in charge," and students who carry the label of "oppositional defiant disorder" (ODD) know it perhaps even better than their peers. What they don't know is how to assert control over their own sense of self, how to express (or recognize) their need for support in learning how to self-regulate, or how to balance their need to feel heard, respected, and understood with a teacher's need for all the same things.

By the time a student has been given the label, they have time and time again failed to meet our expectations, both spoken and unspoken. And we have failed to meet their expectations of us as teachers—that we will see beyond the behavior in front of us, respond to the needs of and respect the autonomy of the child who is showing it. To do so requires a strong belief that behavior is a form of communication, a willingness to try to understand what is being communicated, and an inclination to respond to students with empathy.

When it comes to students identified as having ODD, it also requires the ability to remember that they *are* still children and we are the adults who need to respond as such, something that can be hard to do when we feel personally attacked or offended by their form of communication. It's all too easy to respond punitively or to meet perceived disrespect with more of the same. But, as author Amelia Bowler reminds us, respect and respectful behaviors are both subjective and cultural, and not recognizing that students may not share our beliefs or understand the implicit (if it's not explicitly named) serves neither student nor teacher well.

---

1   Amanda Morin is the associate director of thought leadership and expertise at Understood, a former classroom teacher, and author of a number of books, including *The Everything Parent's Guide to Special Education* and *What Is Empathy?*

In this book, Bowler doesn't shy away from naming the difficulties teachers face and acknowledging the frustration they feel. Still, she accomplishes the daunting task of reminding us that the students whom we find hardest to teach, those whose behavior may lead us to believe they need our support and approval the least, are actually those who need our love, care, time, respect, and understanding the most. She asks teachers to challenge their assumptions, confront their implicit biases, and provides the support, frameworks, and approaches they need to move forward in the classroom while leaving those assumptions and biases behind.

The Teacher's Guide to Oppositional Defiant Disorder is the book I needed 20+ years ago when I began my career as an educator, and it's a book every teacher needs on their bookshelf—not just to understand their students, but also to feel equipped to support them without sacrificing their sense of self-efficacy.

Preface

Before writing my previous book, *The Parent's Guide to Oppositional Defiant Disorder: Your Questions Answered*, I was a parent, searching for answers about why the usual behavior management strategies just did not work with my sensitive and outspoken son. We consulted pediatricians and psychologists, and the assessments told us that he met the criteria for oppositional defiant disorder (ODD). Unfortunately, this label offered no clue about what we should do next. At my son's school, the teachers were struggling too. He seemed to slip through their grasp, finding new rules to break every day.

In addition to being a bewildered parent, I was also a clinician who had helped hundreds of families understand their own children and solve tough behavior problems as a team. I had completed a Master's degree in the science of behavior, plus a teaching degree, with additional studies in developmental disabilities, disability rights, and childhood development. Obviously, I was still missing something, so I wrote the book to try to answer some of the questions I just couldn't answer, no matter how many courses I took or books I read. I wanted to know: "What's different about my child?" and "What do I need to do differently in order to be the right parent for him?"

When a clinician reached out to me to ask if I would write a version of the book for teachers, I flashed back to my days as a substitute teacher and classroom teacher. I thought about all the teachers I have collaborated with as a behavior analyst, and the classrooms I have observed. In my mind's eye, I could also see myself as a student: disheveled and distracted, struggling to meet classroom expectations, and quick to push back against any attempt to control me. I agreed to write this book because I remembered how hard it was to be that teacher faced with a student who would not submit to "authority" of any kind. I hope I can share what I have learned, so that more teachers can get to the end of each day feeling a sense of progress and hope. I also remember what it was like to be that child, the one who is endlessly questioning "Why should I?" and looking for ways to get through the day on her own terms. As I wrote, I thought of the children who protest in "difficult" ways, and the children with unmet needs who wish they had the courage to stand up and be difficult too.

This book is not one that I undertake lightly. There are excellent books already on the topic of behavior management in classrooms, and resources for teachers who want to motivate and engage their students. I began writing this book in order to challenge misconceptions about children diagnosed with ODD, pulling together research on emotional regulation, trauma, motivation, autonomy, executive functioning skills, behavior analysis, and rapport-building. As I wrote, another priority emerged: confronting the over-use of pressure tactics and control-based strategies. Control-based strategies are extremely common in many different cultures, used by everyone, from homes and schools to businesses and courtrooms, but they come at a cost. I have tried to explain exactly what it costs us when we rely on control-based systems, and point to ways we can collaborate with and regain the trust of children who have been hurt by those systems.

Introduction

As a teacher, you may meet hundreds of students, but every so often, one particular student will come along and baffle you. For better or for worse, the most memorable students are often the ones who oppose you at every turn. This antagonism can curdle into daily tension, it can cause you to question your profession altogether, or it can be the start of an extremely rewarding (albeit challenging) relationship.

This book is devoted to investigating these memorable, feisty, impossible, determined students. This book is about the students who refuse to be ignored, who never back down from a fight, the ones who are impossible to overlook. Whether or not an official diagnosis of oppositional defiant disorder (ODD) is assigned to these students, theirs is a challenge that you must rise to.

Part I: Changing the Way You See Oppositional Defiant Disorder aims to shed light on what sets a child diagnosed with ODD apart from their peers. Students with behavioral disorders or emotional regulation difficulties often arrive in your classroom without the hope of support and understanding, because their struggles are hard to see from the outside. They appear to be angry, rude, cruel, erratic, or stubborn, but not visibly disabled. However, behind the mask of ODD, your student may be hiding severe emotional dysregulation, learning disabilities, social disconnection, family dysfunction, trauma, or anxiety. When it comes to challenging behavior, there is often a contrast between the behavior being displayed and the student's private experience. It can be very difficult to see past the defiance, bluster, cursing, and refusal, and understand what is truly happening underneath. By the time a student diagnosed with ODD encounters you, they have had plenty of experience with disapproval and correction, but relatively few positive interactions with adults in authority.

Part II: Changing the Way the Student Sees You explores how you can build connection and rapport with difficult students, so that instead of being a punching bag or a nemesis, you can demonstrate that you have your students' best interests at heart. By reexamining how power is wielded in the classroom, you will have a chance to assess how to best win the cooperation of your students, especially when you find that you cannot demand it.

Part III: Understanding Your Students' Goals and Needs is all about understanding the individual and contextual reasons for "oppositional" and "defiant" behavior, so you can avoid pitfalls and create effective strategies for cooperating with your students. Although the traditional carrot-and-stick approach to behavior management is probably the most efficient and familiar tactic, it does fall apart every so often, and students who do not respond to this system have historically been considered "willful" or "unmotivated." This section will explore individual differences that make some school expectations hard to meet, and shed light on what might be motivating your students (for better or for worse). You will find strategies to introduce into your everyday practice that reduce the likelihood of behavior struggles and improve motivation so you don't have to reach for a bigger carrot or a bigger stick. You will also find tools to help you create intensive, individual behavior interventions when needed.

Part IV: Worksheets will give you the opportunity to reflect, brainstorm, and discuss the most important topics in the book. These activities have been designed so that teachers can engage with the ideas in the book in a personal, practical way, either individually or during a training workshop. *The access code to download these worksheets is SBPTLHN.*

INCLUSIVITY AND ACCESSIBILITY

All too often, behavioral expectations are set according to neurotypical norms. Children who behave in expected ways are considered "normal," and children who deviate from these patterns are judged to be "oppositional" or "defiant." Throughout this book, I have tried to acknowledge the specific struggles faced by neurodiverse students in a typical school setting. Behavioral expectations are also influenced by beliefs about gender and pressure to conform. In an effort to include students who identify outside the gender binary of "boy" and "girl," this book will use nongendered pronouns such as "they" and "them" when referring to students in general. To ensure that people who have intellectual or attentional disabilities can access the material in this book, each chapter ends with a plain language summary. Plain language writing prioritizes clarity over style, and can improve accessibility for people with low literacy or language barriers too.

PART I

CHANGING THE WAY YOU SEE OPPOSITIONAL DEFIANT DISORDER

What makes a child diagnosed with ODD different from any other student in your classroom? Is there something fundamentally different about this student? Are they born with a trait that drives them to rebel? Perhaps it is the child's parents who are to blame, being too harsh or too indulgent. Can they grasp the consequences of what they are doing, or are they completely impulsive? Part I of this book separates the myths of ODD from reality, with an up-to-date review of what we know about children with this diagnosis, inside and out.

CHAPTER 1

OPPOSITIONAL DEFIANT DISORDER

THE VIEW FROM THE OUTSIDE

A hard stare from the furthest row of the classroom. A row of zeroes on a marking sheet. Another shouting match; the contents of a cupboard scattered all over the floor. Whether or not you have ever taught a student with an official diagnosis of ODD, you probably picked up this book with a specific child (or class!) in mind. You have probably taught students whose names are uttered in the teachers' lounge with a certain tone of voice and an unmistakable eyebrow raise. They are infamous; everyone knows who they are, what they did, and to whom. Just like the term "oppositional defiant disorder," the very mention of these students can trigger an involuntary shudder. Just like the term itself, the conversation around these students is usually focused on their intense and difficult behaviors, not their strengths, their values, or what they have overcome.

To understand a student diagnosed with ODD, it helps to know a little about how the term is used, and how a child may come to be given that diagnosis. While some students have their most significant behavior struggles in the classroom, it is very common for these same students to struggle at home with parents and siblings as well.

WHAT KIND OF STUDENT CAN BE DIAGNOSED WITH ODD?

While any child can wake up on the wrong side of the bed, and certain ages are notorious for temporary bursts of willfulness, these ups and downs are a natural part of development. However, when a child seems consistently angry, stubborn, or resistant, and daily routines devolve into fierce battles, families sometimes turn to their health professional to assess whether they are dealing with a typical developmental stage, or something more concerning.

When a child ignores instructions, flouts rules, talks back, and seems to be in constant conflict with others, it is natural to ask:

What is going on here?
Why is this child being so stubborn, so irritable, and so completely outrageous?
Could it be oppositional defiant disorder?

Other questions that might come up include:

> What am I doing wrong?
> Is this child mentally ill?
> Are the parents tolerating this behavior at home?
> Is this child being manipulative and deliberately provoking?

When problems are severe and resistant to change, adults often want to know: What makes this child different? Why is this happening? Is there a label or psychiatric diagnosis that can help me understand what's going on here? In these cases, most parents start by asking their family doctors for advice. Doctors are sometimes reluctant to make outside referrals based on behavior, especially if the child is not obviously defiant in the doctor's office, or if reports from teachers and other caregivers are inconsistent. Many tantrums and struggles can be brushed off as "normal kids' stuff" or chalked up to incompetent parenting. Even cultural differences can make it hard for families and doctors to see eye-to-eye, because what is unimaginable in one community might be quite understandable in another. However, if the family and the doctor can agree on the need for further testing, then a diagnosis of ODD can be queried.

Once a health professional has completed a medical history check and a physical examination, they will interview the family and review reports from other caregivers, taking into account the child's development, health, emotional wellbeing, academic performance, and family situation. They will also look to rule out health problems such as vitamin deficiencies or developmental delays, mental health problems such as depression and anxiety, or neurological differences such as autism and attention deficit hyperactivity disorder (ADHD). If disruptive and challenging behavior persists despite treatment in these other areas, then the clinician may decide to diagnose the child with ODD.

A diagnosis of ODD does not help us to understand the character and needs of the child, or what they have experienced in their lifetime. Still, it is useful to know exactly what the label means. The symptom list for ODD will vary depending on which diagnostic manual is being used. As of this writing, the American Psychiatric Association's (APA) *Diagnostic and Statistical Manual of Mental Disorders*, 5th Edition (DSM-5) is the standard in North America, while the World Health Organization's *International Statistical Classification of Diseases and Related Health Problems* (ICD-11) is used in other parts of the world.

The typical core symptoms of ODD include:

- Persistent defiance and irritability
- Possible aggression and spitefulness
- Outbursts and conflicts happening more frequently than would be expected from a typical child of that age.

In other words, children diagnosed with ODD are thought to be:

- Constantly getting into fights with other students
- Always doing the opposite of what is asked
- Resisting any kind of authority
- Quick to criticize others and to speak rudely
- Acting as if above the rules
- Refusing to take responsibility for mistakes, and blaming others
- Always wanting their own way
- Incredibly stubborn
- Only cooperating when they want to.

When the child is given the psychiatric label of ODD, the diagnosis describes how the child's behavior is understood and experienced by others. A diagnosis of ODD can be validating for family members or teachers who have struggled when the usual checklist of behavior strategies falls short.

Unfortunately, a diagnosis alone does not offer much in the way of answers for parents or teachers. A descriptive diagnosis such as ODD does not explain how and why that behavior developed in the first place. In fact, many people hear the label "ODD" and assume that it is the child who is "disordered," not just the behavior. ODD is then treated as the "cause" of the difficult behaviors, that is, "It's just their ODD." However, this assumption creates a circular argument: Why do they behave this way? Because they have ODD. Why do they have a diagnosis of ODD? Because they behave this way. ODD does not actually explain the behavior at all. A clinical diagnosis of ODD *does not refer to a specific difference or deficit in the child.* The label only describes what we can see.

As you have read, students diagnosed with ODD come with many different skills and struggles. The list of "symptoms" is long, but a child does not have to meet every one of the criteria to receive a diagnosis. The result is a kind of mix-and-match, grouping children who have very different cognitive and emotional profiles together, simply because their behavior looks the same from the outside. A diagnosis of oppositional defiant disorder does not point to a cause. In other words: *oppositional defiant disorder is an incomplete description, not an explanation.*

Ultimately, it is the clinician who must decide what kind of behavior is "normal" for a child, considering any factors that seem relevant, such as culture, gender, and developmental level. This determination is entirely subjective. You might be surprised to learn that there is no agreed-upon tool for measuring what is within the range of "normal" child behavior. A clinician may use a tool such as the Child Behavior Checklist (CBCL) to measure the observations of parents and teachers, and compare these scores to the suggested guidelines, but these guidelines do not provide a yardstick that measures "average" or "normal" behavior in every community (Sandberg & Yager 1991).

COMMON TREATMENT APPROACHES FOR ODD

Once a medical professional confirms the diagnosis, children may or may not have access to a course of treatment. The most common intervention recommended for children diagnosed with ODD is parent training. Manualized programs such as The

Incredible Years® and Triple P (Positive Parenting) have been developed specifically to improve compliance and decrease escalation at home, and research has demonstrated that these programs are somewhat effective (see, for example, Murray, Lawrence, & LaForett 2018; Nowak & Heinrichs 2008). Not all families have access to these programs in their community, and waitlists for publicly funded services can be lengthy. At school, resources for children diagnosed with ODD are often reserved for the most severe cases. School supports may include access to a "calm-down room," time set aside with a resource teacher, or occasional counseling with a social worker, but very few schools have dedicated staff to support students with behavioral issues, and often these interventions work to contain the behavior instead of treating it. Pharmaceutical interventions have also been shown to be effective for some children, especially when there is a co-morbid diagnosis of ADHD, but treatment guidelines for the medical management of ODD are vague, and doctors have limited evidence with which to weigh the risks and benefits of prescribing medications such as stimulants, alpha-agonists, and anti-psychotics.

In an educational setting, a diagnosis of ODD could be helpful for administrators who apply for funding for additional supports, but too often children encounter an eclectic mix of techniques and disciplinary responses as they progress through their education, instead of a well-designed and individualized treatment plan.

ODD AND INDIVIDUAL DIFFERENCES

When you meet a child diagnosed with ODD, you may be able to safely assume that this child probably has a school disciplinary record and a colorful reputation, but children diagnosed with ODD can be very different from one another. They have wildly varying:

- Performance on cognitive testing
- Academic skills
- Family backgrounds
- Home environments
- Health and other conditions.

What follows are descriptions of four different children, each with different gifts and needs, each of whom could be currently classified as having "oppositional and defiant" behavior.

ELLA

Ella has been described as a "free thinker" and a "spirited child" for most of her life. Her parents report that as a toddler she was much less likely to follow instructions than other children her age. She rarely walked hand-in-hand with her parents, and would sometimes leave the playground unexpectedly when her parents took her to the park. When her first-grade teacher suggested a psycho-education assessment, her parents agreed to pay for it. The psychologist's report found no indication of developmental delay and suggested enrolling her in a program for gifted and talented students. Despite her obvious intelligence, Ella seems annoyed when asked to complete her school assignments, and has told her teachers to just leave her alone.

ROSS

Everyone in the neighborhood knows Ross's name, even before they meet him. When his parents take him to the playground, he runs ahead, zigzagging into the road and back onto the sidewalk. His parents call out "Ross! Watch out!" but when they catch up with him, he has already climbed to the roof of the play structure and looks down at them, laughing. While other parents sit together to sip coffee and chat, Ross's parents do not take their eyes off him, and mutter sheepish apologies every time he pushes or trips a smaller child. Ross's parents have even had his hearing checked because he seems to be so oblivious to the warnings and admonitions they give. Ross seems to make friends and gain admirers among his peers wherever he goes, and seems to be very confident. However, many of these friendships sour when his friends try to play imaginative games because Ross plays too rough. He prefers competitive games, but resorts to cheating and making threats if he fears he might lose.

AVA

On the first day of primary school, when the other children were putting on their new school clothes and smiling with smoothly combed hair for "First Day" snapshots, Ava hid under the bed. Her parents eventually persuaded her to go to school, but she still bursts into tears whenever the teacher asks her to share her favorite play materials with others. She often sits along the side of the gymnasium floor during physical education class, complaining of a stomachache. Ava tells her parents that other children tease her at school. She says she can hear them talking about her behind her back, so she keeps her distance. However, Ava's teacher disagrees and hasn't seen any kind of teasing in the classroom, just some giggles when Ava is refusing to go out for recess and shouting at the teaching assistant. At home, Ava's parents have also noticed that Ava gets terribly upset when they ask her to come to the dinner table, and these outbursts sometimes escalate to hitting, screaming, and breaking her brother's toys.

LOUIS

Louis usually comes late to school, after the mid-morning break, looking unkempt and sleepy. Some days, he puts his head down on his desk and ignores his classmates, but on good days he will try to engage them in conversation on his favorite topic: computer games. If his classmates try to change the subject, he interrupts them and talks over them, explaining the latest update or equipment at length. Louis reports that he often stays up extremely late to play computer games, and then "can't wake up for school" in the morning. Louis's academic performance is worrying, but it has been hard for teachers to assess his skills because he misses so much school. However, Louis's biggest problem is his temper. If he feels offended by a teacher or a peer, he can get very agitated, knocking over desks and making graphic threats of violence. Communication with Louis's parent is scarce, though his parent has agreed that it is hard to set limits with Louis at home, especially with regard to video games, chores, homework, and personal grooming, and sometimes they are forced to give in.

WHAT IS THE FUTURE FOR THE TERM "OPPOSITIONAL DEFIANT DISORDER"?

ODD is currently classified in psychiatric diagnostic manuals as a "disruptive behavioral disorder." When you hear the term "disruptive behavior," what do you think of? The definition may vary from teacher to teacher, since behavior that would be disruptive in a math class would be quite appropriate in a physical education class. There are dozens of possible answers to this question, but all of them describe behaviors that are likely to be undesirable, if not downright dangerous. If you were told to expect a new student who was sometimes disruptive, you might want to know: How often is the student disrupting class, and what does it look like? What kinds of situations are likely to trigger this behavior? What kind of supports will be effective? In other words, you would need a more precise description of your student to be able to respond appropriately.

Similarly, clinicians have proposed changes to the term "oppositional defiant disorder" so that the label describes the problem in a more helpful way. Just as post-traumatic stress disorder (PTSD) is now clinically recognized, and terms like "neurosis" and "hysteria" have been set aside, perhaps future versions of psychiatric diagnostic manuals will describe the symptoms of ODD in a different way. Fortunately, psychiatric labels are reviewed and often revised as new versions of the diagnostic manuals are published.

To meet the current criteria for a diagnosis of ODD, a child must display some (but not all) of the behaviors on the list of "symptoms." The list includes three different types of behaviors, and researchers have suggested that these behavioral dimensions could be known collectively as "irritable" (sensitive, easily upset), "headstrong" (determined, impulsive), and "vindictive" (easily offended, attempts to get back at others when provoked.) Redefining ODD by specifying a dimension or subtype could be helpful for researchers who are looking to find out which treatments are most effective.

Symptoms of oppositional defiant disorder can be grouped into three main dimensions:

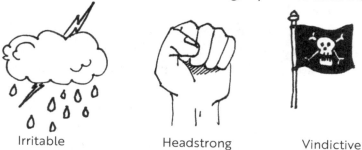

Irritable   Headstrong   Vindictive

Not all symptoms are required for diagnosis; various combinations are possible:

Vindictive, irritable   Headstrong, irritable   Headstrong, vindictive

Some clinicians even argue that ODD should be classified as a disorder of emotional regulation (Cavanagh *et al.* 2017), not simply a behavioral or externalizing disorder. These terms are, of course, still a reflection of how the child's behavior is experienced by other people.

Using the words "irritable" or "headstrong" might help to describe the difference between a child who cries easily and a child who argues frequently, but as descriptive terms, they ignore all the life factors that can contribute to those behaviors, such as:

- Problem-solving skills
- Emotional coping skills
- Executive functioning skills
- Adverse life experiences
- Genetic traits
- Family environment
- Neurological structures.

In other words, a description of the behavior does not always tell us *why* the behavior is occurring and what can be done to help. Research studies and questionnaires rarely capture what the child is experiencing, so to understand ODD, we must be prepared to listen closely and put ourselves in their shoes.

OPPOSITIONAL DEFIANT DISORDER AND THE SCHOOL EXPERIENCE

ODD is often discussed as a problem that affects families, but a student diagnosed with ODD will frequently struggle to conform to the expectations of the classroom environment as well. Schools are very structured environments, and students are asked to follow many different rules and instructions throughout the day, without negotiation or complaint. Any kind of refusal or disruptive behavior will obviously have an impact on a child's educational experience. However, the connection between learning and disruptive behavior is complicated and often bi-directional. In other words, challenging behavior can interfere with learning opportunities, and learning difficulties can lead to challenging behavior. Students who are restless and strong-willed may find other ways to pass the time during lessons. In many cases, students who persist in off-task or disruptive behavior are asked to leave the classroom or barred from certain activities.

The link between disruptive behavior and missed learning opportunities is evident, but the converse is also true: students who are already academically behind may push back on school expectations in general, and become anxious when asked to take part in challenging activities. Learning difficulties such as dyslexia or auditory processing disorder can go hand-in-hand with difficult behavior too (a diagnosis of ODD does not strictly imply any kind of intellectual disability, although they can occur together). In some cases, a pre-existing problem can affect both a student's self-management skills and their academic learning opportunities. If a student is struggling with poor self-control, heightened sensitivity to stress, or lack of problem-solving skills, these factors can increase the risk of aggressive behavior as well as contribute to a student's struggle in the learning environment.

Here are some examples of what a child struggling at school might tell us:

Teachers never like me, so I might as well have some fun.

I'm always tired. I can never sleep properly.

I'm hopeless at school. Why bother trying?

I really don't see the point of any of this.

All I really want to do is talk to my friends. They understand me.

I can't stop thinking about that argument with my mum.

This room is so loud and smelly. Why do I have to be here?

Please don't call on me. I can't remember anything you just said.

This teacher is a control freak, and doesn't care what I think.

I wish I could talk to someone I trust.

This doesn't make sense. Why are we doing this?

Why should I stop doing this, just when I was actually enjoying myself?

Is this teacher trying to intimidate me? Has he got something to prove?

If I have to hear one more complaint, I'm going to completely lose it.

It just annoys me when people bark orders at me, so I ignore them.

ACADEMIC PROBLEMS AND BEHAVIORAL OUTCOMES

For some students, specific academic problems (such as poor reading skills) seem to predict behavioral difficulties later on (Miles & Stipek 2006). Frustration and anxiety can certainly spark refusal, or perhaps an underlying attentional disorder may be at the root of both academic difficulty and behavioral problems.

Unfortunately for teachers, many of these learning problems can go undetected in children who are adept at avoiding academic demands, and a diagnosis of ODD does not specifically imply a lack of ability or intelligence. The diagnosis can be given with or without another label such as a learning disability or mental health disorder. In either case, behavioral problems and academic difficulties are often tangled up together. When a student is chastised and corrected for behavior at school (see, for example, Garwood, Vernon-Feagans, & Family Life Project Key Investigators 2017), they may protest by refusing to work. If a student is overwhelmed with frustration during lessons, they may become disruptive and hostile.

As you proceed further into this book, you will find strategies for engaging disruptive students, improving your relationship with them, and drawing them back into a cooperative relationship, regardless of their academic abilities.

SUMMARY

This book is for teachers. Some of your students may be diagnosed with oppositional defiant disorder (ODD). Doctors give a diagnosis of ODD to children if they argue a lot with their parents, tease others, and do not listen to instructions from adults. No one knows exactly why some children act this way. There are probably many different reasons. Some people think that children diagnosed with ODD are naturally rude, or that their parents did not teach them to listen, but this is not true.

Children diagnosed with ODD are not so different from other children. It is normal for children to cry, tease, and disagree with their parents sometimes. In some communities, parents and teachers expect children to follow strict rules. Other communities allow children to argue and disagree. Doctors give a diagnosis of ODD if they think the child is disobeying more often than other children in that community. When children cry, tease, ignore, and disagree a lot, parents and teachers get frustrated. They want to understand what is happening, and figure out how to get along together.

Children diagnosed with ODD often get into trouble at school. Some children get distracted or upset when they do not understand what you are teaching. Other children are already distracted or upset, so they miss the chance to learn.

The label "oppositional defiant disorder" does not help parents and teachers understand how to fix the problem. ODD is not a mental illness or a physical difference. It describes what the child does, but it does not explain why the child does it. In the future, doctors might choose a different name for "oppositional defiant disorder." If doctors choose a better name, then parents and teachers will be able to understand what kind of problem the child is having, and how to help them.

CHAPTER 2

STRUGGLES LINKED WITH OPPOSITIONAL DEFIANT DISORDER

Research shows that children diagnosed with ODD may also accumulate a number of other psychiatric diagnoses (Nock *et al.* 2007), including depression, anxiety, ADHD, intermittent explosive disorder, learning disabilities, and conduct disorder. Other studies have pointed to a higher risk of ODD among certain groups with particular family structures, parenting styles, or socioeconomic status. However, most research studies point to a correlation but cannot show how those variables are really connected. Most available psychological research is carried out examining large groups of subjects and looking at the patterns that emerge. It is a daunting task to separate all these labels, and even harder to use this information in a constructive way.

For instance, if you learned that a certain percentage of children diagnosed with ODD have an unstable family home, some have a history of psychiatric disorder in the family, and some have parents with a mood disorder, what would you do with this information? Statistical information is of limited use because generalizations about ODD *may not apply to the child in front of you*, and furthermore, they do not suggest a useful course of action.

There are many different circumstances and conditions that can contribute to the main struggles of a child diagnosed with ODD, but they can be broadly categorized by type. Most children diagnosed with ODD are struggling in at least one of the following areas:

- Emotional self-regulation, including emotional reactivity, coping skills, and physiological processes
- Executive functioning skills, including self-control, attention switching, focus, and planning
- Social problem-solving, including self-advocacy, perspective-taking, and communication.

EMOTIONAL REGULATION AND DYSREGULATION

For many children diagnosed with ODD, emotional self-regulation is a significant problem. The clinical description of ODD includes descriptions of "frequent anger" or "touchy" behavior, which implies a genuine emotional roller coaster.

Changes in mood or attitude are to be expected, of course, and there is no objective measure as to whether an emotional expression is appropriate, but a student can be considered to be *emotionally dysregulated* if either of the following is true:

- They violate social norms in their expression of those emotions, or
- Their emotional ups and downs are getting in the way of them reaching their personal goals.

Emotional self-regulation is such an important topic that it is *easy to forget that it has only recently become a valid subject of scientific study*. Only a generation or two ago, children who cried and screamed were considered "badly behaved" (and probably "poorly brought-up" by their parents), and children who complied with a smile were thought to be "well behaved" (with parents to be congratulated for their excellent discipline). We now know that the process of emotional self-regulation involves an interplay between physiological changes, thoughts, relationships, settings, sensory experiences, and behaviors. Upbringing does, of course, have a part to play, but there are many other factors that can influence a child's emotional self-regulation.

In fact, emotional self-regulation is closely linked with the other two areas mentioned above: executive functioning skills and social problem-solving. Poor executive functioning skills or inadequate social problem-solving skills will certainly put a strain on emotional self-regulation, and conversely, a child who is emotionally dysregulated cannot fully access executive functioning skills or engage in social problem-solving.

On its own, emotional dysregulation can be defined as the inability to adjust one's emotional responding to within an "acceptable" range. Usually, an onlooker would judge the "acceptable" range of emotion expression depending on context, such as situation or age. For example, sports enthusiasts watching a game would not be considered *dysregulated* for shouting and screaming in the stands, but the same behavior would not be tolerated in a library. The ability to regulate one's emotions is a complex skill that takes many years to develop. Children rely on trusted caregivers to help them "co-regulate," and they often need help interpreting their own body's signals.

This simplified description of the process of emotional self-regulation outlines all the steps in the chain reaction of emotional responding, involving a person's physical environment, some subtle and immediate responding in the brain, a cascade of hormonal responses, deliberate reasoning and perception, the social environment, available actions, and learning history.

The process of emotional self-regulation involves the following, in some order:

A change in the environment	An emotional response usually starts with a change in the environment. This change can also be a personal one, such as a physical sensation or even a thought.
Ensuring safety	Neuroception is another word for the brain's ability to detect risk. Almost instantly, any small change is assessed and determined to be a possible opportunity, a threat, or nothing of interest. Some neuroceptive responses are unconditioned, such as feeling startled by a loud noise. Experience and exposure can also lead to conditioned responses, so that the "threat detection" process is triggered by a sound, smell, or situation that has been associated with unsafe situations in the past (Griffin *et al.* 2020).
The body responds	The detection of an opportunity or threat triggers an increase in the level of physical "arousal" (e.g., increase in heart rate, skin reactivity, pupil dilation). Increases in arousal such as curiosity, anger, or fear are triggered by the *sympathetic nervous system.* In moderation, this kind of arousal is associated with feelings of excitement, courage, suspense, and motivation. Acute stress responses may be helpful in survival situations like running from a burning building, but in the wrong context, they can also result in panic attacks, aggression, and over-reactions. The stress response resolves when the *parasympathetic nervous system* brings respiration, heart rate, and other functions back into balance.
Thoughts that shape feelings	Meanwhile, thoughts and perceptions shape the meaning and impact of this change. People often "hear" their own thoughts as verbal behavior, using labeling and perspective-taking to make a threat seem more manageable. Self-talk and coping statements can help to change the intensity of the initial emotional reaction. Thoughts can also put the situation into context (Guinther & Dougher 2015), such as: "Worse than..." "Better than..." "Just like..." "Yet another example of..."
Relating to friends or foes	Social context can have a strong impact on a person's emotional experience, depending on who is nearby and how they respond. The presence of other people can: • Offer cues as to what emotional response is socially acceptable • Influence *threat perception via body language and facial expressions* (Porges 2011) • Change cognitive assessment by making a problem seem more manageable • Change cognitive assessment by making a problem seem more threatening • Offer opportunities for coping behaviors.
Making a move	Taking action can help with emotional self-regulation: • Looking around to see if help is available can change the social context • Taking deep breaths can trigger soothing physiological changes • Moving away from the problem can change the threat perception • Confronting and resolving the threat can influence emotions • Practice and training can help suppress unhelpful impulsive responses.

As you can see, emotional self-regulation is not an entirely reflexive or voluntary response; it is an interplay between voluntary and involuntary processes.

When a child is emotionally escalated, it's easy to assume that the child is:

- Lacking in proper training and discipline
- Rude, aggressive, and belligerent
- Intentionally hostile toward those in authority
- Trying to gain an advantage.

In fact, resistance and aggression toward authority figures can mask a surprising vulnerability. Some students are more sensitive to stress than others, and this sensitivity can be expressed in different ways. Newborns differ in their ability to respond to and recover from stress. The strength of this response depends on the activity of the vagal nerve (sometimes known as stress vulnerability or "vagal tone"; see Porges 1992). This neurological process helps to explain why some children, even from a very early age, are hard to soothe and require a lot of extra care.

As these children grow, they retain a certain sensitivity that can make it hard for them to discern between a real threat and a minor inconvenience. When this child enters your class as a student, they may experience anxiety, confusion, or frustration, which can be displayed as anger, criticism, or rebellion. The external display of belligerence hides the fear and worry underneath. The psychologist Mona Delahooke describes this tendency as "faulty neuroception" in her book *Beyond Behaviours* (2020). Loud and aggressive behavior can sometimes mask anxious feelings, as the student's stress response floods their body with hormones that prepare them for "fight, fight, or freeze."

Of course, a student who feels anxious or unsafe is not always loud and hostile. They may also respond by trying to avoid or withdraw from the situation, issuing a flat refusal, spinning out a lengthy negotiation, or simply putting their head down on the table and refusing to speak.

If a child is overestimating the danger posed by a difficult situation, other areas of difficulties can easily become emotional landmines. Students with learning disabilities may take extreme measures to avoid academic tasks. If the student has difficulty making and keeping friends, social situations can set off a storm of emotions. Situations with intense sensory input (if the student has sensory processing difficulties) can make everything else feel like an imminent threat.

ENVIRONMENTAL FACTORS AND COPING SKILLS

In terms of the physical and social environment, children do not have much control over what goes on around them. They are confronted with experiences that are uncomfortable and confusing. Later in life, people gain the option to make changes to their environments to support their emotional wellbeing, such as moving to a different neighborhood, switching jobs, or choosing friends, but children do not have much influence over what happens to them.

As a typical child develops, there will be "stages" where they face new challenges, and their coping abilities are outpaced by their new possibilities. The most notorious developmental stages include "the terrible twos" and the onset of puberty, where children are learning to separate themselves from their parents in new ways, but have not quite found a sense of security or stability. However, for some children diagnosed with ODD, their coping abilities always seem to be a few steps behind the challenges they face. They seem easily stressed and overwhelmed, quick to over-react or lash out.

Managing stress is never as simple as "making good choices," as there are many different factors that can make a child more vulnerable to stress.

Risk factors for stress vulnerability	Examples
Stressful environments and Adverse Childhood Events (ACE)	Family conflict (Fergusson & Horwood 1998), addiction, crime, poverty, instability, isolation, abuse, or mental illness can take a heavy toll on a child. When a child is bombarded with environmental stressors, they are constantly "under threat." Chronic stress can have a negative impact on both physical and mental health.
Physiological changes; difficulty recovering from stress	"Polyvagal theory" suggests that a child's vulnerability to stress is partly determined by the vagus nerve, which mediates cardiac and respiratory functions, among other things. Babies with poor "vagal tone" take longer to recover from situations of high arousal. In children and adults, poor "vagal tone" can make it more difficult to switch attention, respond flexibly, and use coping strategies, because they are "stuck" for longer in that physiological state (Skowron *et al.* 2013).

Some neurological traits (including autism and ADHD; see Morris *et al.* 2020) have been linked to differences in the ability to process sensory information or extreme sensitivity to changes in their environment. For example, Autistic children appear to be very alert to change (Sinha *et al.* 2014), so in some environments they are constantly scanning for possible danger. A burst of emotion is also a common symptom of ADHD.

When children have difficulty moderating high or low levels of sensory input, they show more physical signs of stress (e.g., higher cortisol levels in their saliva) (Reynolds, Lane, & Thacker 2012). When a person is on "high alert" for threats, their bodies are primed for action. When a person is in this defensive state (sometimes known as the fight, flight, or freeze reaction) all resources are directed toward survival. Less essential skills, like the ability to laugh at jokes, think creatively, or empathize with others, are temporarily blunted.

Other sources of stress, such as pain, hunger, loneliness, and lack of sleep, can interfere with the body's ability to self-regulate. Traumatic experiences can also interfere with a person's ability to detect a threatening situation from a safe one. |

Cognitive vulnerabilities and executive functioning skills	As noted above, a child who is already in a state of distress will have difficulty accessing skills that help with emotional self-regulation, such as logic, impulse control, reasoning, planning, and perspective-taking.
	Similarly, any event or condition that affects cognitive functioning, executive functioning, and reasoning skills can also have an impact on emotional self-regulation, including:
	• Fetal alcohol effects • Developmental disabilities • Acquired brain injuries • Genetic differences, such as fragile X syndrome • ADHD • Neglect or malnourishment.
	When children have difficulty switching attention, shifting perspective, and imagining other possibilities, they are more prone to distress and less able to cope with challenges. This problem may help to explain why children diagnosed with ODD who also have poor executive functioning skills appear to be more prone to a later diagnosis of generalized anxiety disorder and major depressive disorder (Drabick *et al.* 2011).
Lack of social support	A child first develops emotional self-regulation in the context of a relationship with their caregiver. Children who have the benefit of warm, responsive parenting are much more likely to have good emotional self-regulation skills.
	When a parent cannot self-regulate or respond appropriately to a child in distress, this escalates the child's emotional dysregulation. When parents regularly respond to their children with a dismissive, harsh, or sarcastic reaction, those children are more likely to grow up with a clinically significant disruptive behavior disorder.
	(For a powerful demonstration of how children look to caregivers for help with emotional regulation, see video examples of the "still face" experiment, e.g., Barbosa *et al.* 2021.)
	A lack of appropriate social support can result in:
	• Maladaptive strategies for gaining adult attention • Difficulty interpreting nonverbal communication • Missed opportunities for learning empathy and perspective-taking via a model • Missed opportunities for learning through coaching and suggestions for coping behaviors.
	It is also important to note that in some cases, children receive warm and responsive care but do not benefit as much because they are overwhelmed with stress responses, for reasons mentioned above. In other cases, children in distress do not get the benefit of support responses because they express their emotions in unexpected ways. For example, if a child who is privately experiencing intense distress instead appears to be withdrawn, angry, menacing, suspicious, bitter, mocking, sarcastic, hyperactive, or even giddy and laughing, adults may not pick up those cues and respond in a helpful way.
Limited behavioral repertoire	Emotional self-regulation involves taking action to resolve the problem in some way.
	If children do not have role models who demonstrate good coping skills, they will have limited options for resolving their emotional distress. Their "fight response" will tend to be the default because it is so well practiced, while other possible responses, such as requests for help, are not rehearsed, prompted, or modeled.
	Additionally, if adults tend to respond to a child's emotional outbursts by immediately giving in to the child's demand or removing an unwanted expectation, the emotional dysregulation becomes an adaptive strategy for problem-solving.

Although children do not choose their physiology, and cannot choose the events they face or the people around them, they can acquire problem-solving strategies that will help them cope. This type of learning often depends on safe and supportive relationships with caring adults.

SENSITIVITY TO SOCIAL REJECTION

Rejection-sensitive dysphoria is a term that describes intense distress in response to perceived social rejection. Social rejection is never a pleasant experience, and most people cringe at the thought of being excluded, accused, or criticized by their peers. Scientists have found that social rejection can trigger the same parts of the brain that register physical pain (Eisenberger, Lieberman, & Williams 2003). In other words, rejection hurts. Since social rejection is such a predictably upsetting experience, studies of emotional dysregulation are often designed using social exclusion tasks. For example, participants could be invited to play online games with an unseen partner while researchers measure the participants' response when the unseen partner starts to exclude them or treat them unfairly.

For some people, the pain of social rejection is easily triggered by subtle things that would go unnoticed by other people. This group of people might interpret a small and unintentional gesture as a cruel jab, or read between the lines of an email to find a message of humiliation. This sensitivity is especially common among people diagnosed with ADHD, although rejection-sensitive dysphoria has not yet been added to the list of ADHD symptoms in a diagnostic manual like the DSM-5.

Social rejection and stress reactions go hand in hand. When a student is socially rejected, they are likely to experience a burst of activity in the cortisol centers of the brain, as stress hormones are released throughout the body. Students who are already experiencing stress tend to be more sensitive to the possibility of social exclusion.

For some students, rejection-sensitive dysphoria develops from a history of experiencing correction, exclusion, and shaming from others. Students who are especially impulsive tend to attract a lot of negative feedback, as do students who do not easily conform to social norms. Other students may over-react to social feedback simply because they are already stressed. Sometimes social exclusion does not trigger a noticeable outburst, but it can be part of a chain of events that leads to an emotional or aggressive meltdown later on.

OPPOSITIONAL DEFIANT DISORDER AND FAMILY STRESS

When students come into the classroom with poor self-control and a mistrustful attitude, it's easy to blame the student's family. After all, most online health resources will tell you that ODD is associated with harsh or inconsistent parenting, adverse life events such as divorce or abuse, or heritable personality disorders and learning difficulties:

Where did she learn that kind of language?
I can't believe his parents let him get away with that.

Their parents have to tell them that this is not acceptable.

However, the relationship between challenging behavior and family stress is a complicated one. In other words, parents of children diagnosed with ODD might be more prone to harsh or inconsistent parenting tactics, but it would not be fair to assume that that the child's behavior patterns have been *caused* by poor parenting. A child's behavior is certainly influenced by their parents' choices, but studies (see, for example, Barkley & Cunningham 1979) have shown that a parent's behavior is certainly shaped by the way the child responds. If the child doesn't react when the parent gives gentle reminders or mild corrections, a parent might naturally try to push harder or back off (more on the "coercive cycle" later).

Similarly, when a child grows up in a deprived environment, such as a home with parents who cannot care for them consistently, who suffer from mental health problems, or who have experienced abuse and trauma themselves, they miss out on important learning opportunities for emotional coping and problem-solving. However, parents who raise a child with high needs will also experience additional strain. For example, if a child is often excluded from school, parents may struggle to work enough hours to make ends meet, or face pressure at work when they are forced to take time off. Parenting a child with high needs can pose a significant strain on relationships (Wymbs *et al.* 2008). Even individually, parents of children with high needs often struggle with depression and anxiety, an understandable response to being responsible for others in a volatile and even violent environment.

OPPOSITIONAL DEFIANT DISORDER AND EXECUTIVE FUNCTIONING SKILLS

The term "executive functioning skills" refers to a set of cognitive abilities such as memory, planning, visualization, and regulating attention. Highly developed executive functioning skills are required for logical thinking and self-control. Poor executive functioning skills are associated with impulsivity, disorganization, and irritability. Clearly, if a student struggles with self-control and emotional self-regulation, this would place them at risk for more outbursts and conflict with others.

If you were to test the executive functioning abilities of a large group of students diagnosed with ODD (Kleine Deters *et al.* 2020), you would find that even among students who had similar rates of challenging behaviors, the results would range from very poor to very high. Poor executive functioning does not correlate exactly with behavior problems, but it does help to predict some outcomes (Cristofani *et al.* 2020). For example, students with less developed executive functioning skills are more prone to emotional dysregulation and reactive (e.g., sudden, unplanned) aggression. They are also more likely to develop major depressive disorder (Dickson, Ciesla, & Zelic 2017) and generalized anxiety disorder. Indeed, there are children who struggle with impulsivity and self-control most of the time due to neurological differences that affect executive functioning (this group would include children who have ADHD, brain injuries, and some genetic differences such as fragile X syndrome).

However, there are some children who appear to be able to function well, stay organized, and keep out of trouble until some emotional stress is introduced. In one study (Schoorl *et al.* 2018), children diagnosed with ODD (but without a diagnosis associated with poor executive functioning skills, such as ADHD) were given a test of executive functioning skills along with a group of typical peers. Their scores were similar, up to a point. When the students were given a series of frustrating games to play, and then had their executive functioning skills retested, researchers found that the students diagnosed with ODD suffered a greater impact on their scores than the typical children. This result might suggest that being sensitive to frustration makes it harder for students to retain the logical and orderly skills that usually help them. When emotional self-regulation skills are vulnerable, the ability to problem-solve and think creatively in stressful moments is compromised and harder to deploy.

Students with more developed executive functioning skills were also at risk of aggressive behavior, but this aggression was more likely to be planned or deliberate (Thomson & Centifanti 2018). Students with better executive functioning skills were also more likely to go on to be diagnosed with conduct disorder rather than mood disorders (Pardini & Fite 2010).

ATTENTION DEFICIT HYPERACTIVITY DISORDER

Deficits in executive functioning skills are a defining feature of ADHD. Given that ADHD affects approximately 5 percent of the population (Sayal *et al.* 2018), you have almost certainly had students (and co-workers) who would fit the diagnostic criteria. Among students diagnosed with ODD, the prevalence of ADHD is much higher (at least 50 percent). In other words, ODD is frequently diagnosed among children with ADHD, and vice versa.

To understand ODD, it is essential to have a thorough knowledge of ADHD and its impact. Unlike ODD, ADHD is classified as a neurodevelopmental disorder. It is often inherited and usually lifelong. Children with ADHD tend to be impulsive, highly active when motivated, curious, and drawn to novel things. They also have difficulty with emotional self-control, and find it quite hard to stay focused on unappealing tasks, or to switch their attention away from activities that interest them. Sensory-seeking behaviors are common among children with ADHD, possibly to help soothe when over-stimulated, or satiate when under-stimulated.

Typical symptoms include:

- Deficits with working memory
- Impulsivity
- Difficulty with emotional self-control
- Sensory-seeking behaviors

- Difficulty staying focused
- Difficulty switching attention.

A child with ADHD may find it hard to meet school expectations, such as sitting still, taking turns speaking, completing long tasks, and staying calm in large groups. This frustration and lack of inhibition can certainly contribute to some of the disruptive behavior associated with ODD. Given that about half of all children with ADHD qualify for a diagnosis of ODD (Noordermeer *et al.* 2017), we can assume that problems with emotional self-regulation and executive functioning present a major (but not impossible) challenge for them.

CONDUCT DISORDER

By the time a student's behavior is diagnosed as "oppositional" and "defiant," there has likely been some rule-breaking involved. However, if a student's behavior escalates to the point where it could be described as dangerous and antisocial (specifically, behavior that infringes on the rights of others, such as setting fires, assault, or threatening others with a weapon), the student may be given a diagnosis of conduct disorder—at least 30 percent of children diagnosed with ODD will go on to be diagnosed with conduct disorder as well (Nock *et al.* 2007). Conduct disorder is considered an "externalizing behavior disorder," like ODD, but the two diagnoses are different in one important way: "oppositional" and "defiant" behavior tends to happen in relationship with other people, and often includes an emotional escalation. The behavior associated with conduct disorder is not always relational or emotional, and can take place when no one else is around. If your student seems to be quite emotionally stable and a good problem-solver, but is already in the habit of rule-breaking, this can present its own set of challenges for a teacher. If rebellion and defiance are the most effective ways to make friends and meet goals, then this type of student is at a higher risk of escalated rule-breaking associated with conduct disorder such as arson, burglary, or premeditated assault later in life.

PUTTING THE PIECES TOGETHER

So far, we have looked at most of these risk factors for ODD one at a time, but in reality, many of these problems are interconnected. For example, your student's executive functioning skills might seem typical on a good day, but you notice they completely fall apart when they start to feel frustrated. Your student's emotional dysregulation problems may lead to frequent meltdowns and missed learning opportunities, which contributes to social isolation, loneliness, anxiety, and depression.

Students who struggle with emotional self-regulation need safe, solid, sensitive support. Stress can even displace the motivation to learn. Without emotional self-regulation, your student is less able to think creatively, solve problems, and see the perspective of others. Stress can even displace the motivation to learn. Without emotional self-regulation, your student cannot perceive logical and natural consequences.

A student who is experiencing a stress response will have difficulty being flexible, considerate, patient, or resourceful. Students learn self-regulation within the context of safe relationships. Adults help the process along by noticing and responding to small changes in the child's thoughts and emotions. Initially, children rely on others to suggest ways of coping and to offer the assurance of comfort and safety. As you respond to a student in distress, you demonstrate for them what empathy looks like. You teach through your listening skills, your body language, and your problem-solving approach.

SUMMARY

Every day, you feel many different emotions. Some emotions make you want to shout or dance or run away. If your emotions are strong, it might be hard for you to do your job or talk to other people. Emotional self-regulation helps you control your feelings.

Emotional self-regulation has many different parts. Your brain helps you detect danger. Your body helps you get out of trouble. Your thoughts help you understand the problem and decide what to do. If you have safe people around you, those people can help you stay calm and find a solution. If you have solved similar problems in the past, you can use what you have learned.

If you are missing some of these things, emotional self-regulation will be harder for you. You might feel like there is always danger around. Your body might start acting before your brain starts thinking. You might not understand the problem. You might not have safe people around you. If you have not solved a similar problem, you may feel confused and upset.

- Some children diagnosed with oppositional defiant disorder (ODD) have difficulty controlling their emotions. They get upset easily, and have difficulty calming down. They do not feel safe with other people, and they want to make their own decisions.
- Some children diagnosed with ODD have difficulty with planning and self-control. They sometimes forget the rules and get distracted. They get stuck thinking about one thing. These children pay attention to "right now" and think less about "later."
- Some children diagnosed with ODD have difficulty getting along with other people. They make mistakes when they try to guess what other people are thinking. They do not know what to say when other people are upset. These children feel alone and scared because they do not know how to ask for help. They also feel like other people do not like or accept them.

All of these problems can be connected. For example, if your student has difficulty controlling emotions, they might also find it hard to think clearly and connect with other people when they feel upset.

These problems are common for people diagnosed with attention deficit hyperactivity disorder (ADHD). Many children who are diagnosed with ADHD will also be diagnosed with ODD. Later in life, many children diagnosed with ODD will also be diagnosed with depression and anxiety. Some children start to break more serious rules, and doctors give them a diagnosis of conduct disorder.

CHAPTER 3

CULTURAL COMPETENCE, MISUNDERSTANDINGS, AND BIAS

To be able to respond to your students, it helps to understand their behavior in the context of culture. This type of sensitivity can help you to notice and interpret a change in your students' language, posture, or body language. What counts as "defiant" or "rude" behavior, anyway? If you answered this question and compared your results with the person sitting beside you, the two answers might be quite different, depending on your respective gender, socioeconomic class, sex assigned at birth, country of origin, and religious tradition. It is hard to come up with an exact definition of defiant behavior, but most people would agree: "I know it when I see it."

Unfortunately, when there is no agreement, there is plenty of room for misunderstanding. Even the word "defiant" is loaded with malice and evil intent. When you interpret a behavior as "defiant," you feel "defied." However, the same behavior could inspire pity, empathy, or even admiration when viewed with a different lens.

Consider this quote from a teacher attempting to explain the difference between children who "behave" at school and children who do not:

> ... things that would cause positive behavior in school: I would think would have to do with parents. If they have a good family background where there's respect for people in the family and they're expected to behave for their parents. And when they come to school, they just tend to fit right in, if they come from a family where there is social interaction and expectations of managing behavior. (Quoted in Dutton Tillery *et al.* 2010, p.92)

What kind of behavior looks like "respect" to this teacher? What would make up a "good family background"? Where would these students "fit right in"? What assumptions might this teacher make about a student who does not behave as expected? What could this teacher assume about the student's family? As your cultural competence grows, you will be able to look outside your own experience and your own community norms, to bring context and compassion to students who appear to be "oppositional" and "defiant."

37

CULTURAL COMPETENCE

Your personal definition of "offensive" behavior is determined largely by the culture that surrounds you. Your community has expectations of how many questions a student should ask, and what it means when a student asks "too many" or "not enough" questions. Your community has standards for how much eye contact is considered friendly and appropriate. In excess, a person could be judged as menacing, and if they give too little eye contact, they are considered aloof. Your community assigns meaning to a smile from a stranger, but whether that stranger is seen as a fool or a friend is a matter of geography.

This section mentions some specific differences between communities as examples but will not adequately cover the topic of cultural competence and neurodiversity. If your school offers training or continuing education opportunities on the topic of inclusion and anti-racism, take the time to participate. After all, we don't know what we don't know, so it is important to seek out other perspectives. Reaching out to elders and community leaders can also be a powerful way to learn about the specific communities you serve.

Defiant, deviant, or diplomatic? Some advice on communication in context

Communication	Practices for inclusion and sensitivity
Eye contact	Be flexible in how much eye contact you give or require. Too much eye contact is threatening in some cultures, and uncomfortable for some Autistic people. If your student has difficulty with eye contact, set up your conversations in such a way that you both have another focal point, e.g., sitting side by side, coloring on a piece of paper.
Emotional expression and energy	Some cultures place value on the ability to speak in a lively and animated way. They may associate enthusiasm with sincerity. Other cultures show respect by choosing words carefully and using an even tone. If you and your student are on opposite ends of this spectrum, you may feel a disconnect when you try to communicate. Be aware of your expectations when it comes to expressiveness, and do not pressure your student to match your style.
Facial expressions	Be prepared for some unexpected facial expressions, and try not to jump to conclusions. A student who smiles after being reprimanded by the teacher might not be signaling defiance. Instead, smiles are used in some cultures to indicate embarrassment and shame. Also, social smiles are often exchanged between strangers in North America, but elsewhere in the world, a stranger who smiles is not to be trusted.
Jokes and teasing	In some cultures, teasing is an important way to express affection or group acceptance, even to adults in authority. Consider context before you respond, and if you can react with good grace, you may have just increased your social standing with the group. Be mindful of how you use humor with students too. Sarcasm and self-deprecation are extremely common in some cultures, but a witty remark could fall completely flat in the wrong context.
Small talk	Conversation, including chit-chat and small talk, is highly valued in some cultures, but be mindful that some cultures are extremely comfortable with silence. In Finland, for example, they say: "Silence is golden, talking is silver." Canadians, on the other hand, will strike up a friendly chat with the cashier or even compliment a stranger at the bus stop on their stylish coat. This kind of outspoken quality is highly valued in some communities, but elsewhere it would be considered quite unexpected or even unnerving.

RACIAL DISCRIMINATION, STEREOTYPING, AND INEQUALITY

A diagnosis of ODD is given based on how parents and teachers rate a child's behavior, and ideally, these ratings would be objective and reliable. Unfortunately, people are prone to making errors in reporting and interpreting the behavior of others. Differences in culture, race, faith, gender, and age can increase the risk of misunderstanding, stereotyping, and discrimination. These misconceptions and assumptions have very real and dangerous results (too numerous to fully describe here) in the workplace, in healthcare, in the economy, and in schools (Harris *et al.* 2006).

When discrimination occurs, it is not always the result of explicit or even implicit bias (Mitchell 2018). There is no attitudinal test that will predict whether you will discriminate unfairly or not. Whether you personally hold discriminatory beliefs or not, your decisions can still be influenced by unjust policies and incomplete information. Your choices should be weighed up in light of the fact that your students will face discrimination in many forms (Gregory, Skiba, & Mediratta 2017).

Bias and inequality in behavior assessments

The effects of discrimination can easily be seen when children come into contact with disciplinary procedures (Fabelo *et al.* 2011). Studies of school disciplinary referrals show that school employees are more likely to treat certain groups of children as threatening or disruptive, and to assign them heavier consequences (Gopalan & Nelson 2019).

Discrimination can also affect who is singled out for a referral to the special education class (Serwatka, Deering, & Grant 1995), and who is given a behavioral disorder diagnosis. In your role as a teacher, you may be asked to fill out reports for psychiatric evaluations and to answer questions about the child's behavior. These answers are evaluated by the psychiatrist and compared with parent reports. Questionnaires that measure student misbehaviour in relative terms such as "often," "hardly ever," or "most of the time" are more easily swayed by racial bias against non-white students. However, this bias is not as evident when questionnaires invite teachers to state the frequency of misbehaviour in specific terms (e.g., "1–2 times per day" or "3–4 times per week"). You can also bear this in mind when you read a student's file and review psychiatric reports written with feedback from other people who are just as susceptible to errors like these.

Addressing racial bias in school rule enforcements

Cultural differences can also contribute to misunderstandings, unfair punishment, and personal conflicts. School rules often enforce cultural standards of modesty, style, and communication that single out students of color. School rules against headwraps, twists, Afros, or dreadlocks are mainly enforced against students of color. Some school rules even explicitly forbid mouth noises common in African and Caribbean communities, such as "kissing teeth" (or "le tchip") (see McPartland 2015.) Even when rules apply across the whole student body, studies have shown that non-white students suffer due to a disparity in rule enforcement.

According to a report presented by the Government Accountability Office (GAO) to the US Congress (Nowicki 2018), Black boys and girls were much more likely, compared to White, Hispanic, and Asian peers, to be disciplined for misbehavior at school. When the researchers factored in poverty and compared groups with similar socioeconomic status, this difference persisted. Researchers investigated further by reviewing disciplinary cases in specific schools where the Office of Civil Rights had found instances of discrimination, for example, different punishments routinely given to students for *the same infractions.* For example, in some cases, Black students were much more likely to be given suspensions or school exclusions, while White students were given warnings or in-school detention.

As a result of the investigations, the schools attempted to improve their disciplinary policies in a variety of ways:

- Implementing Positive Behavior Support or Restorative Justice policies
- Clarifying district rules regarding exclusionary disciplinary practices
- Prohibiting the use of corporal punishment and isolation rooms
- Improving support services for students.

Confronting racism and discrimination in your school will require systemic change and continued effort. If you teach in an American school, you will find a list of key federal resources for guidance and support within the GAO's report (Nowicki 2018). If you are looking for support to improve equitable treatment for marginalized groups in your school, you may find similar resources in your country, at the federal or local level.

FACTORS THAT CONTRIBUTE TO DIFFERING RATES OF OPPOSITIONAL DEFIANT DISORDER DIAGNOSES

The diagnosis of ODD is relatively rare in some communities, but a difference in diagnosis rates does not reliably reflect a difference in rates of disruptive behavior. There are many reasons why the label of ODD may be over- or under-diagnosed, such as:

- Cultural traditions that stigmatize psychiatric evaluations and mental health labels
- Racial biases and prejudices that lead doctors and educators to perceive more aggression and defiance compared to children with different backgrounds but similar behaviors
- Accessibility of services such as behavior therapy, counseling, and medication
- Quality of education, nutrition, and other social programs that support healthy communities.

SUMMARY

In the classroom, students and teachers show each other respect with their body language and words. When you see your student acting in a way that does not look respectful, you feel offended and uncomfortable. People show respect in different ways when they are from different cultures. People from different cultures or backgrounds may have different expectations about how to show respect. They have different ways of looking at each other, speaking, standing together, making jokes, and sharing information. This is also true for people with different neurotypes. If you understand a person's culture and neurotype, you will be able to understand their body language and words without being offended by the differences between you.

Teachers are not always fair in the way they treat their students. Teachers sometimes give more punishment to Black students even when their behavior is the same. When doctors and teachers write behavior reports for children, they often make the Black children sound more dangerous and difficult than other students. These doctors or teachers may not realize that they are treating Black students differently. They may not have unkind thoughts about Black people as a group. If you want to treat your students more fairly, you can measure behavior by choosing one simple action to look out for, and counting how often it happens, then compare it to other students. Avoid guessing.

CHAPTER 4

MANAGING YOUR FRUSTRATIONS AND EXPECTATIONS

In 2018, a survey conducted by the Policy Exchange asked teachers in the UK: "Are you currently, or have you previously, considered leaving the teaching professional because of poor pupil behavior?" Twenty-four percent of respondents answered "yes—currently" while 26% of respondents answered "yes—previously" (Williams 2018, p.32).

As a teacher, disruptive student behavior can make a lesson feel more like a battle. A rude remark can shatter the mood, distract the other students, and sometimes even get under your skin. Some disruptions are harder to detect, but it is tiring to be vigilant and keep everyone on task, feeling like someone is always trying to steer you off course.

A teacher of a student diagnosed with ODD may say:

Why does she hate me so much?

I actually dread walking through the door of my classroom this year.

Some days aren't too bad, but most days are just so draining.

I never know what is going to set them off.

I just asked her to do one simple thing and everything just spiraled from there.

He's okay in my class, but I keep getting called in to de-escalate a crisis at lunch or in other teachers' classes.

As soon as I turn around, she's scribbling on the desk or tearing pieces out of her notebook—anything but actually doing the work.

The other students avoid him, because he has a reputation for getting too rough and saying the most inappropriate things.

I've never seen a student so determined to refuse. Sometimes I can hardly finish the question before they are telling me 'No!'

She knows I can't physically make her do it, and she takes advantage.

Nothing seems to make any difference. I can't get through to this one. I can't make them want to learn.

It's really hard on the other students to have to deal with all this disruption. It's not fair to them.

ESCALATING BEHAVIOR PROBLEMS AND DISCIPLINARY MEASURES

Getting help from outside the classroom can be frustrating. While some students may respond to a stern talking-to from the principal, and some are anxious to avoid a call to parents, many students diagnosed with ODD end up facing a series of escalating consequences that do not address the underlying problem. Without effective intervention, these students often end up removed from the classroom temporarily, then returned without making amends, or barred indefinitely from the school environment.

This problem is especially common in schools where the behavior management approach:

- Relies on reactive strategies instead of proactive support
- Is mainly punitive
- Does not clearly indicate which students should be referred to specialized teams
- Does not provide active support until the student is already in crisis
- Does not provide assessment that analyzes possible functions of the behavior.

In one study examining the use of Functional Behavior Assessments (FBAs) in schools (Ross 2017), teachers reported that of the 13 cases where they requested a referral to a behavior analyst, many were for student behaviors that were "unmanageable," "disruptive," and "dangerous," but no proactive strategies had been attempted in any of the cases. In 12 of the 13 cases, reactive strategies such as privilege loss, reprimands, sending the child to the school office, parent contact, and suspension were tried, but evidently without success. Eventually, standard behavior management at a school led to all of the identified students being suspended by the middle of Term 1. One student was suspended for 30 of the first 39 days of school.

The reasons for referral were even more heartbreaking: only a handful of teachers referred their students for an FBA in the hope of understanding the challenging behavior. A larger percentage of the teachers reported that they were simply looking for a way to remove the child from the classroom.

If you recognize yourself in this chapter, or you see similar problems in your own school's disciplinary policies, keep reading. This book will point you to evidence-based strategies that you can use in your classroom, and resources and training topics that you can suggest to your school's administration.

TEACHER ATTITUDES AND STUDENT OUTCOMES

To put it frankly, it's hard to appreciate a student who is disruptive, aggressive, grumpy, and volatile. It is completely natural to prefer students who are cooperative, industrious, and agreeable.

However, teacher preference is a powerful variable that can influence a child's social standing (White, Sherman, & Jones 1996) and academic achievement. Research has shown that a change in teacher preference can influence a student's social standing, increasing or decreasing peer rejection. A warm teacher relationship can boost academic achievement even in the years that follow. For decades, researchers and educators have wrestled with the question of whether high student achievement is linked with high teacher expectations. In other words, will a teacher's beliefs about a student become a self-fulfilling prophecy? The answer to this question has not been easy to discern, because researchers have not been able to replicate this phenomenon reliably in experimental studies. There has also been strenuous debate about how exactly these variables are linked, for example, how do teacher expectations influence their behavior in the classroom? Do teacher expectations have an impact on a student's self-concept? Does self-concept influence achievement?

To keep from getting lost in this maze of theory and assumption, let us review what we know for sure:

- As teachers, we develop expectations and opinions about our students.
- These expectations and opinions will influence the way we treat our students.
- We will probably communicate some of these expectations and opinions to our students.
- Students will form opinions about us.
- Students will even form opinions about our expectations for them.
- Some of these expectations and opinions will probably turn out to be unfounded.

When it comes to expectations and student achievement, high expectations do not always result in high achievement (Jussim & Harber 2005), for some fairly obvious reasons:

- To provide effective scaffolding (adaptive, contingent support), the teacher must have a realistic assessment of student abilities (van de Pol, Volman, & Beishuizen 2010).
- Students thrive on meaningful feedback that helps to celebrate success and to adjust performance (Ferguson 2011).
- Students who are told "I believe in you, you have great potential" will continue to struggle if they do not also have accessible learning opportunities and meaningful feedback.
- Explicitly emphasizing a student's potential can actually damage motivation (Dweck 2008), because students will try not to take risks that could lead to errors that might expose their weaknesses, to protect the ideal story of their "potential."
- If a teacher sets expectations that are too far beyond the student's abilities, the student will struggle to meet those expectations.

EXPECTATIONS REDEFINED: THE POWER OF OPTIMISM

Expectations are important, and they absolutely do shape behavior. Even though "high student expectations" are not quite the hoped-for solution, your attitude and thoughts have a significant influence on your "real life" behavior. According to the principles of cognitive behavior science, your thoughts are basically a lens through which you view the world. Your thoughts help to predict what you will take note of, what you will take action on, and what opportunities you seize. An attitude that is *realistic, yet hopeful* is probably the ideal outlook for a teacher. You recognize the challenges in front of you, but you see the potential for improvement. In other words, you maintain an *optimistic* outlook.

Dr Martin Seligman's research on optimism contributed much more than the "glass half-empty or full" analogy (2006). Seligman's work identified some of the specific thoughts that support good mental health, adaptive functioning, and even physical health. He found that optimistic and pessimistic people make different kinds of predictions, because they have *different beliefs about the world*. Seligman called these two sets of beliefs "explanatory style."

Specifically, the difference between "optimism" and "pessimism" can be found in how you answer the following three questions:

- Is this my fault somehow?
- Is everything always going to turn out this way?
- Am I stuck like this?

	Optimist	Pessimist
Is this my fault somehow?	"There are lots of factors to consider. It's not just about me." Belief: Problems happen in context, and are not connected to fixed traits.	"I'm just not meant to do this, and I'm not good at this type of thing." Belief: There's something wrong with me.
Is everything always going to turn out this way?	"Life is full of surprises, and I think we can still turn this around." Belief: Most problems are temporary, not permanent.	"This type of thing happens to me all the time. Might as well get used to it." Belief: It has always been like this and it always will be.
Am I stuck like this?	"I can work on this, one little piece at a time." Belief: Problems can be addressed gradually.	"The problem is just too huge. It's overwhelming." Belief: It's all or nothing. Most things are too big and complicated to really change.

Fortunately, these optimistic habits of thought can be learned through practice, and studies have shown that people who practice optimism as a skill do see improvements in their mood. Furthermore, people who practice optimistic thoughts are more likely to show resilience in challenging times, and to take the initiative in improving their circumstances. Dr Mark Durand demonstrated this by inviting two groups of parents to undergo behavior management training (2011). Both groups of parents had children with very challenging behavior, but the group who went through optimism training (in addition to behavior management training) was more likely to carry out the recommended procedures, was more successful in their efforts, and there was even a comparative improvement in the behavior of their children.

Teachers face all kinds of challenges in their workplace, and optimistic thought habits can help to stave off feelings of frustration and helplessness. Optimistic teachers acknowledge what they cannot change, but they look for opportunities where they can make an impact.

SEE THE STRUGGLE, FIND THE STRENGTH

Students diagnosed with ODD are known for their ability to stir up trouble, stoke chaos, and make a fuss. They defy norms and sometimes they even literally break things. Their behavior is not just difficult: it also *tends to offend*—that offensive quality is part of what defines the label "oppositional defiant disorder." If a student's behavior did not offend other people, it would not be called "oppositional" or "defiant." It would be called anxious, inattentive, talkative, opinionated, determined, strong-willed, developmentally delayed, or something else entirely.

Unfortunately, this offensive quality also repels people. It undermines sympathy and fails to evoke pity. In other words, it is hard to imagine helping a student who seems to be set against you.

When Dr Ross Greene wrote the influential book, *The Explosive Child* (1998), he proposed a radical mindset shift for parents and teachers of children with oppositional behavior (Greene & Ablon 2005). He suggested that instead of looking at disruptive behavior as something to be conquered and eliminated, adults could approach difficult behavior as a form of communication. In other words, adults can learn to look at difficult behavior and remind themselves:

*They're not giving me a hard time. They're **having** a hard time.*

Although this attitude is a hard one to adopt, especially for parents and teachers who are already stressed and exhausted, it does open up a new set of possibilities.

This mindset can help adults shift their behavior from defensive to supportive, even when enduring a verbal tirade or a literal barrage of fists. The words "I hate you" can be understood as something else, like "I need you" or "I don't understand you." A torn-up worksheet is not just an act of academic sabotage; it can also mean "I'm scared." In other words, "offensive" behavior doesn't have to offend us (unless we let it).

As you take on a more compassionate perspective when confronted with oppositional or defiant behavior, you will be able to see different opportunities for intervention. When you look at the angry or contemptuous child with the same curiosity and concern that you would offer a child who was ill with a fever, or sad after a fight with a friend, you can set aside the urge to blame or shame.

CULTIVATING POSITIVE FEELINGS TOWARD HARD-TO-LIKE STUDENTS

For some students, a caring teacher can make all the difference. Having a warm and supportive relationship with a teacher can make it easier for high-risk students to ask for the help they need (Ryan, Gheen, & Midgley 1998). A strong positive connection empowers you as a teacher: it makes your praise and your feedback more valuable to your students.

Just as the psychologist Dr Greene encouraged parents and teachers to see students' struggles as vulnerabilities and areas of need, a social worker named Bertha Reynolds advocated for what she called a "strengths-based approach." This can help to balance out your view of your students, so you can see more than just their deficits and needs.

The strengths-based approach

Dr Martin Seligman, a former president of the American Psychological Association (APA), affirmed this approach in an address to his colleagues: "The most important thing we learned is that psychology was half-baked. We've baked the part about mental illness, about repairing damage. The other side's unbaked, the side of strength, the side of what we're good at" (1999).

Of course, the classroom is not the ideal place to identify the strengths of some students. Their very best jokes might be told in the hallway instead. Their grace and determination might be easier to spot on the sports field. Their kindness might be more visible on the weekend, when they visit their grandma. If you are looking for more reasons to like your student, but you are seeing only sullen glares when you smile at them, you can start by looking at your student's struggles in a new light.

Often, our strengths and our struggles are two sides of the same coin. Here are some strengths that don't always translate easily to the classroom. See if you can recognize some of these strengths in your most challenging students:

- *Determination:* A determined student will take on a challenge and see it through, even though it requires making unpopular decisions.
- *Curiosity:* A curious student will test everything, and explore every possible outcome, finding learning opportunities even when you haven't planned one.
- *Courage:* A courageous student isn't afraid to speak out, to try new things, and to stand up to a challenge. They will often do the thing everyone else wishes they could do but doesn't dare. Sometimes the biggest risk leads to the best rewards.
- *Leadership:* A student with leadership qualities can command attention from others, speak up with passion, and is not swayed by peer pressure. Rather, they share their own ideas and influence others to follow.
- *Passion:* A passionate student student doesn't do anything in half-measures. Whatever they choose to do, they do it wholeheartedly and with commitment. Often, these students are excellent advocates for others, against injustice. Life is never boring when they are around.
- *Honesty:* An honest student is forthright, and doesn't waste time with much tact or hesitation. If you have a piece of spinach in your teeth, you can count on them to let you know (instead of snickering about it behind your back). You never have to wonder where you stand with them.
- *Integrity:* Sometimes truth can get lost in the grays between black and white, but not for a student with integrity. Even if it means doing something awkward or

costly, they will stand up for what they think is right, and follow through on their word, even when circumstances change. Excuses, white lies, and social niceties are no reason to break trust or depart from this student's cherished values.

- *Logic:* A logical student appreciates understanding the "why" and carefully thinks through their actions. Not prone to impulsive behavior, rule-bending, compromise, or people-pleasing, this student tries to be consistent and correct above all things.
- *Creativity:* Although a creative student might not do what is expected when you hand out classroom materials, you can't help being impressed by how many other uses they can find for a single object. Unbound by tradition or even common sense, this student can bring ingenuity and surprise to just about anything.

SUMMARY

When students break rules in your classroom, you might feel very frustrated. You might want to avoid students who do not cooperate with you. In some schools, the only way to fix a problem between students and teachers is to move the student to another classroom. Even before finding a way to change your students' behavior, you can try to change your thinking. When you remember that your students are young and full of possibilities, you will be able to see more of the good things they do. When you remember that your students are also feeling uncomfortable, you will have warmer and kinder feelings about them.

You can even change the way you think about your students' behavior. Optimism and pessimism are different ways of explaining what you see. Optimistic thinking helps you to keep trying even when things are hard. Pessimistic thinking makes problems seem bigger than they really are.

Optimistic thinkers do three important things:

- They look at the whole situation.
- They solve problems one small piece at a time.
- They remember that situations can change quickly.

Instead of focusing on the mistakes your students make, you can try to look for reasons to celebrate your students and their strengths. Even when they are not listening to your instructions, they might be showing you something they can do well. For example, a student who points out your mistakes might be unusually good at telling the truth. A student who argues with you is also standing up for what they believe. When you decide to pay attention to what your students do well, this is called a "strengths-based approach."

ATTITUDES OF A SUCCESSFUL TEACHER:
A NOTE OF ENCOURAGEMENT FROM
ONE TEACHER TO ANOTHER

Disclaimer: While most of this book was written with reference to the current research literature and in consultation with experts, this section was written based on the author's personal experience and beliefs. It is more "teacher's lounge" than "textbook," but you may still find it useful.

As teachers, we are advised not to "take it personally" but...

When we are ignored, we may feel insignificant.
When we are struggling, we may feel weak.
When we are refused, we may feel defied.
When we are accused, we may feel defensive.
When we are insulted, we may feel belittled.

All of these emotional reactions are natural and understandable, but we can choose to respond differently. Instead of taking things personally...

When a student is not responding...we can give them time.
When a student is not going along with our plan...we can give ourselves time to think and adapt.
When a student says "no"...we can try to learn more about why.
When a student misunderstands or criticizes...we can demonstrate the truth.
When a student uses harsh or untrue words...we can look past the words with curiosity and empathy.

PART II

CHANGING THE WAY THE STUDENT SEES YOU

Once you have seen past the mask of "oppositional" and "defiant" behavior, you will be able to see your student with more empathy. You can even cultivate more appreciation for the students who have so far been hostile and hard to like.

However, your student may take some time to warm up to the idea of an alliance with you. After all, by the time you meet them, they have years of experience being pressured, coerced, warned, corrected, and pushed in a school environment, and they will probably expect the same from you.

CHAPTER 5

CONTROL AND AUTONOMY

As a teacher and a leader, your challenge is to find a way to work with your students, not against them. While some may be willing to go along with you by default, students diagnosed with ODD are no stranger to resistance and conflict. If you give an instruction to a student diagnosed with ODD, they may ask, "Why should I?" In this section, you will have a chance to prepare an answer to that question that does not rely on the exertion of authority.

Your student probably already has a response to some of the typical flexes they have encountered in the past:

Common pressure tactic	"Defiant" response
"Do it because I said so."	"I'm not afraid of consequences." "I don't see the logic." "I'd rather have my freedom." "I have other priorities."
"Do it because you'll get a reward."	"You're going to ask me to do something I hate." "I don't want to be forced." "It's not worth the effort." "If I tell you what I want, you're going to withhold it from me." "I don't want to go along with your agenda." "Can I trust you? What if I do it and I don't get the reward?" "If you think you can handle me with rewards, then I assume punishment is right around the corner too."
"Do it or there will be a punishment."	"I can handle your punishment." "I'll punish you right back." "I can avoid your punishment." "I can make sure it's not worth your while." "I don't appreciate being threatened."

Speaking of being pushed, your student is probably quite familiar with waging power struggles. If you choose to change that power dynamic, you will have to unlearn some old tactics. The switch doesn't happen overnight. It will take time for both of you to reset and practice new ways of interacting. Engaging with adults in a collaborative way can be particularly difficult for students with a history of trauma. Your student will need some cues from you to confirm that you are a safe, well-intentioned person, so this section is written with the trauma-informed approach in mind.

CONTROLLING SYSTEMS

In a controlling power dynamic, the person in authority decides what should be done and when. The rest of the group (those without authority) is expected to obey. In exchange for their submission, they may gain the approval of the person in authority, they may win some agreed-upon prize, or they may simply avoid the unpleasant consequences of disobedience. A person's acceptance into the group depends on their willingness to follow the instructions of the person in authority. This framework is common in many cultures and institutions, and you might recognize it from your own upbringing or school experience.

In both schools and clinical settings, the "manage-and-discipline" model prevails (Armstrong 2018). Here are some of its core assumptions:

- Behavior as a fundamental phenomenon can be quantified and controlled.
- Children's behavior can be reduced to variables that can be manipulated and managed.
- Given the right skills and training, the teacher can have complete technical control over the classroom behavioral environment.
- Teachers require the technical and professional skills necessary for students' behavioral compliance.
- Those who do not respond to this exercise of power are unmanageable—a threat to the orderly classroom.

The controlling power dynamic is simple, it is familiar, and it "works," to a certain extent. If the person in authority has the group's best interests at heart, and the group is willing to accept and go with the flow, then the system can be sustained. If a group member pushes back against the system, incentives and punishments are then used to pressure them back into compliance. For example, the person in authority can use preferred items and privileges to distribute selectively among the obedient group members, or insist on an escalating series of unpleasant consequences to discourage dissent and maintain control. If the group members have their needs met within that controlling system, or if they are willing to trade their personal goals for a chance at the rewards on offer, they tend to keep participating in that system.

If your training and experience are similar to most teachers, then you have had some training in behavior management strategies, perhaps in the context of a "special education" class. In the classroom, many behavior management strategies are based on the ability to earn or lose a valuable privilege, including stickers, ice cream, access to preferred activities, access to recess, and free time (Dutton Tillery *et al.* 2010). Teachers can hand out incentives to individuals or to groups of students when they meet or exceed classroom expectations. Similarly, rule violations can be marked by verbal reprimands, demotions on a clip chart, or writing names on the board, usually resulting in the loss of privileges and escalating to more serious consequences if the rule violations continue.

In the classroom environment, "good behavior" is usually defined in terms of how closely the students follow instructions. When asked by a researcher to define "positive behaviors", one teacher described it this way: "on task behaviors...completing assignments, doing what's asked, obedience, I think obedience to authority" (quoted in Dutton Tillery *et al.* 2010, p.92).

Obviously, there are some significant drawbacks to the controlling power dynamic as a basis for a classroom. When group members don't have their needs met, or they don't respond to the incentives and pressures in the system, they tend to stop participating or they start protesting against it.

When your student experiences abuse or neglect within a controlling system (such as a dysfunctional family, foster caregiver, or school environment), they are likely to resist being part of a controlling system again, even one led by a benign or friendly figure. Even when a controlling system is set up with smiles, "positive reinforcers," and minimal "punishers," your students may be reluctant to opt in. They may interpret any kind of controlling system as unsafe after experiencing a feeling of powerlessness and a loss of trust. When you look at these students from a trauma-informed perspective, you can see that their resistance and "defiance" is not simply a need for control, but a need for safety.

"OPPOSITIONAL" BEHAVIOR AND THE "NEED FOR CONTROL"

When a student challenges the instructions of the teacher or violates school rules, they are sometimes tagged as having a "need for control." In fact, control is extremely valuable to all of us (Ackerlund Brandt *et al.* 2015), so these young "disrupters" are not alone in their desire for it. People will often give up a lot simply for the sake of having a choice. Choices can make painful situations easier to tolerate. The value of control cannot be overstated. In fact, the feeling of *being in control* literally makes hard experiences easier to bear. This phenomenon was demonstrated in the 1970s by researchers administering shocks to unfortunate undergraduate students. When the students were led to believe that they could reduce the duration of the shocks by performing a quick task, these students actually had a different physiological experience compared to other students who simply experienced shorter shocks without conditions (Geer, Davison, & Gatchel 1970). Specifically, the students experienced less stress as measured by skin conductivity tests. Many other (less painful) studies have demonstrated that in the classroom, students who are presented with meaningful choices demonstrate more engagement and learn more (Assor, Kaplan, & Roth 2002).

There is nothing pathological about wanting to have one's own way, but we must all learn how to negotiate with others as we try to meet our goals. When a student takes a stand, what sets them apart is their willingness to take extraordinary steps in pursuit of control. In fact, since the question "Why does this student want control?" is so self-evident, it might be more useful to ask this question: *"Why is this student willing to sacrifice so much to maintain control?"*

CONTROL AND COUNTER-CONTROL

While obedience and compliance are valuable in the context of a group or institution, most people experience "being controlled" as unpleasant. It is not simply the lack of choice that makes these situations aversive. Perhaps it chafes to know that another person is calling all the shots (Ryan & Grolnick 1986). In this sense, the defiant and oppositional students of the world are completely relatable. If we couldn't sympathize with them, we would not watch so many films where the plot centers on a plucky hero who defeats the overbearing tyrant (*Hunger Games*, Harry Potter series, *Independence Day*, etc.).

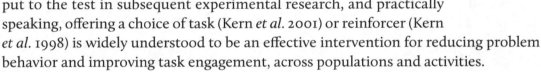

Note: Just an aside to the traditional behaviorists who happen to be reading this book, B. F. Skinner had a lot to say about freedom and control, such as this quote from *About Behaviorism*: "Feeling free is an important hallmark of a kind of control distinguished by the fact that it does not breed counter-control" (1974, p.217). This observation has been put to the test in subsequent experimental research, and practically speaking, offering a choice of task (Kern *et al.* 2001) or reinforcer (Kern *et al.* 1998) is widely understood to be an effective intervention for reducing problem behavior and improving task engagement, across populations and activities.

SUPPORTING AUTONOMY IN THE CLASSROOM

Schools are usually very structured environments, with rules, schedules, and expectations, but fortunately, structure is not equivalent to control. A classroom can be highly organized while still supportive of student autonomy.

Control is about more than just rules and consequences. In a highly controlling classroom, learners are under pressure to obey, to think correctly, and to act *correctly*. The decisions of the teacher are final and arbitrary. Classroom priorities reflect the values of the teacher alone. This description may sound harsh and unkind, but schools tend to rely on controlling systems for good reason—a hierarchical approach has several distinct advantages. For instance, a controlling system tends to be quite stable, whereas cooperative or democratic arrangements are highly responsive. Moreover, a controlling system can operate efficiently, because many people are working toward a singular goal. In a cooperative system, decision-making tends to be more complex and costly, as each choice must reflect several different viewpoints.

The opposite of control is autonomy. Autonomy is often confused with freedom, but a better description would be "meaningful choice." Within the constraints of a classroom environment, students can still find purpose and a voice.

Autonomy is not an all-or-nothing experience. If you have ever flown as a passenger on an airplane, then you have experienced a mixture of constraints and choices. You can choose your destination when you buy your ticket, but you do not plan the route. You can select your seat and you can request your favorite drink, but you cannot nominate yourself to fly the plane. No freedom is absolute. Some restrictions are easy to tolerate, especially the ones that make sense. The most frustrating rules are the ones that seem to have no purpose. On a plane, like in a classroom, control is the most efficient approach, but a degree of autonomy creates a more enjoyable experience.

In your classroom, you do not have to open yourself up to constant negotiation and persuasion in order to provide some autonomy to your students. The best learning experiences are not always the activities that a student would select independently. Maximum benefit does not always spring from maximum choice, and the long-term value of an activity may not be immediately obvious to your students.

Your students can express their preferences and give feedback, but they are not responsible for mapping out the curriculum, and you are not responsible for earning the enthusiastic approval of each student, all day long.

For better or worse, people are complicated. When students walk into your classroom, they bring with them so many different and often competing interests, such as personal preferences, personal goals, community expectations, family expectations, status among peers, values and beliefs, physical needs, and psychological needs. Immediate consequences are not always required to maintain and guide behavior or to manage disruptions. On a good day, these individual factors can help to fortify your students' willingness. However, there will be days when no amount of razzle-dazzle will light up their eyes, and that is to be expected.

In his paper "Autonomy-Supportive Teaching: What It Is, How to Do It" (2016), Johnmarshall Reeve lays out the contrast between what he calls "controlling" classrooms and "autonomy-supporting" classrooms.

Controlling approach	Autonomy-supporting approach
Neglect of the learner's perspective	Listening to students, inviting feedback
Attempting to change the learner's thoughts	Explains rationale, provides information
Pressure applied until the learner changes their thoughts and actions	Provides meaningful choices

Here are some examples of statements used in controlling and autonomy-supporting classrooms (see Reeve & Tseng 2011):

Controlling statements	Autonomy-supporting statements
"Do it this way. Hurry."	"Here's an opportunity to learn more about yourself."
"Your job is to get the right answer. Solve it completely without any mistakes."	"To get you started, here's a hint."
"That's not what you were told to do."	"You're right, this isn't easy."

As you can see, in an autonomy-supporting classroom, the teacher is still in a position of leadership. However, the student is having a completely different experience. The teacher in the autonomy-supporting classroom is giving the student a rationale for the task, without expecting it to be done perfectly. If the student expresses frustration, the teacher accepts and acknowledges this as part of the experience.

The transition from controlling to autonomy supporting can be overwhelming at first, because it runs contrary to so many assumptions and beliefs embedded in our society. We accept controlling systems and take them for granted, even though most of us have experienced the frustration and strain when we lacked control.

Here is an example of how one teacher took a leap of faith toward introducing autonomy-supporting practices into her classroom:

After eight years' teaching the same grade level, Ms Spencer had all of her curriculum materials and lessons expertly organized. Her classroom was tastefully decorated with the right amount of bunting, and parents swooned over her bulletin boards. After attending a workshop on student autonomy, Ms Spencer decided to try it out. After all, her students were getting a little sluggish as the warm weather approached, and there weren't too many more weeks left in the year. A little pedagogical experimentation and increased student engagement were in order.

Her first step toward supporting was bold, but utterly sincere. Standing in front of the class, she announced: "Today, I was hoping to talk about simple machines. It's part of our science curriculum, and I've put together some activities that I think you will enjoy. Does that sound alright with you?" Her students, a little taken aback, mumbled their assent, and Ms Spencer carried out her lesson as usual, but with an extra spring in her step.

On day two, her experiment with autonomy-supporting practices hit a bit of a snag. Once again, Ms Spencer introduced the next lesson on simple machines by explaining her rationale and a possible benefit, and then asked, "How does that sound to you?" She was just about to start handing out the first set of worksheets when Laurence raised his hand. "Miss? It doesn't sound very good to me. I'd rather not."

Ms Spencer froze, mid-stride. For a moment, she stood there, eyes wide. This was unexpected. However, she decided to take Laurence at his word. "Okay, Laurence, thank you for letting me know. Well... I think we'd better talk about this... Gina, can you please hand out these worksheets for me?"

The class was strangely quiet as everyone strained to hear the exchange between Ms Spencer and Laurence. Would she throw him out of the class? Would he be sent home early today? Would she double his homework?

Laurence sat at his desk, digging his nails into his eraser. Ms Spencer crouched down beside him and to his relief, she smiled. She opened the conversation by repeating what she had heard: "Laurence, you were saying that this activity doesn't sound very good to you? Can you tell me more?" Laurence flushed, his voice breaking a little as he admitted: "I'm sorry Miss, but I've done this activity already. I just can't see what more I have to learn from it."

Ms Spencer looked as if she were about to say something, then stopped herself. At last, she began again: "I see what you mean, Laurence. It might be dull to do exactly the same activity again. Yes, that makes perfect sense. Hmm. Well, where does that leave us?"

Laurence brightened a little: "I could walk around and help people read the instructions. Would that be okay with you?" Ms Spencer tried not to smile too widely. "Of course, Laurence, if you wouldn't mind, that would be extremely helpful. It would definitely be more interesting than sitting here doing nothing at all."

On day three, Ms Spencer woke up feeling quite refreshed, intrigued to see what kind of creative ideas her students would come up with that day. She introduced the lesson as usual: "Good morning, class! I have organized a game for us today so we can practice our mathematics. What do you think of that?" Several students nodded in agreement, but some seemed to be smirking. A muffled giggle broke the silence.

Alicia stood up, glancing at her friends, and announced: "Ms Spencer, today I would prefer to eat ice cream sundaes. No math for me, please." She sat back down, covering her mouth to try to hide a triumphant smile.

Ms Spencer wasn't sure how to arrange her face, exactly. In her many years of teaching, she had never heard a student say anything so ridiculous. She couldn't decide whether to laugh, to scold, or to sigh and just carry on with the lesson as usual. After all, it was a lively game and the students were sure to enjoy it.

Ms Spencer was made of fairly tough stuff, however, and decided to give her autonomy-supporting notion a little more time to play out. As with Laurence, Ms Spencer consulted with Alicia privately, and opened the conversation in a similar way: "Alicia, from what I understand, you were thinking you'd rather have ice cream today and skip math altogether?" She paused and watched Alicia's face. Clearly, Alicia wasn't sure how far to take her joke, but she wasn't one to back down easily either. "Yes miss. If I can do whatever I want, I'd like to choose ice cream." Ms Spencer prodded a little further: "And not math?" Alicia shook her head: "No, not math. I think I'm allergic." Ms Spencer smiled a little, and waited to see if Alicia would say more. Alicia had been prepared for a long lecture or a sharp retort, but the silence unnerved her a little. She shifted in her seat. Ms Spencer wondered aloud: "Maybe there's a particular issue with the game?" "I don't even know what the game is," admitted Alicia, "I just don't know why we need to do this stuff at all. It seems pointless to me." "I can't force you to play, so you can sit out if you would like, but I don't have any ice cream today," Ms Spencer replied gently. "Also, you bring up a good point. I don't think I've said very much about why we are learning this type of thing. If you like, I can explain a little more tomorrow, but I see that the class is waiting for me to start the game. I'll let you decide whether you'd like to play or not." The game proceeded, Alicia sat idly for a while but joined in halfway, and Ms Spencer counted this as a win.

It must have been a full moon on day four, or maybe Ms Spencer's lucky streak simply came to a halt. When it came time to open the history textbooks that morning, six hands shot into the air. Ms Spencer looked at the clock, and back at her students. There was simply no time to hear the grievances of six different students and make six different alterations to the lesson. She was stumped.

"I'm afraid I am at a loss here. I'd like to make sure each of you are comfortable with the lesson today, but I don't think I have time to speak to you all individually."

Six hands lowered, and the students looked around at each other. "Okay, boss," one muttered. "Yep," another agreed. "Same old same old." "Let's just get it over with, Miss," called Gwen. Ms Spencer did not budge. She closed the history textbook and set it on her desk. "I don't think I'm ready to throw in the towel yet. I've been enjoying hearing your thoughts. It's been quite refreshing. I think you might have some ideas to make our class better for everyone. Is there a way we can each have our say?"

For the rest of the history period, the class debated the merits of this new approach. "What if someone just always complains and decides never to do any work?" Sun Lee inquired. "Send 'em to the principal's office!" called Adam. "What if I don't want to tell you what the problem is, and I just don't feel like doing it?" asked Kingston. "Do I have to come to school at all? Do I have a choice?" asked Mara. "What if I want to do something, but everyone else thinks it's boring?" worried Lina. "Can we vote on what we want to learn about in class?" suggested Faraz. Ms Spencer listened, and wrote down comments and questions until the bell rang.

That night, Ms Spencer did not sleep so well. However, she had not come so far to simply give up. The next morning, Ms Spencer announced: "I've given this some thought, and I appreciate everything you shared with me yesterday. I'd like to do some more listening, so here's what I'm offering: for the next few weeks, I'll try to speak to at least one person every day, and if you have any objections to the work we are doing, you can tell me then. If you can bring a possible solution to your problem, that's even better! When I've heard your concerns and ideas, we will meet as a group and try to agree on solutions to the problems we are facing. In the meantime, I might not have time during the lesson to hear your concerns, but you may certainly choose to write me a note. I hope you'll participate in our class work in the meantime, because these activities are meant to be valuable to you, and I don't want you to miss out."

Together, the class drew up a list of responsibilities. At the end of class, they had agreed the who, the what, and the why:

Who	What	Why
Ms Spencer is responsible for...	Planning activities and assignments	So we can learn what we need to know at this grade level
	Explaining and problem-solving with students	So we can understand what we need to do
	Offering us challenging work	So we can grow and get smarter
	Listening and caring	So we can get the help we need
Students are responsible for...	Meeting their basic needs (food, water, sleep)	So they can feel good during the day
	Making the best of class time	So school tasks can get done when we are together
	Looking out for the needs of others	So we can be safe and comfortable when we are together

As you can see, autonomy is usually more complicated than control. A less confident teacher than Ms Spencer might have withdrawn the "privilege" of choice when her students used it in unexpected ways. Ms Spencer found that her students were unsure about what to do with the autonomy she offered, evidently worried that their choices might not meet with the approval of the rest of the class, and skeptical that they could really be allowed to have a voice in a school setting. However, Ms Spencer decided to stay curious. She chose to extend the benefit of the doubt to her students without abdicating her responsibility as the leader of the classroom. While listening to her students, she consulted her own values, explained the legal and practical limitations, and challenged her students to consider the needs of the group as well as their own preferences.

Grappling with the consequences of autonomy is part of maturation, and some students will not be ready to participate in higher-level decisions that affect others. However, teachers can share decision-making power with students in many ways, inviting them to give feedback on the style of lesson, pace, seating arrangement, method of assessment, preferred activities, daily routines, etc. When students have the opportunity to exercise control, they can also participate in evaluating the effects of those decisions. Sharing power often means sharing responsibility. If the outcome is poor, the decisions can be reversed, and this type of experiential learning is invaluable for students. When Ms Spencer placed her trust in her students, they responded by putting more trust in her.

As an adult in a leadership role, you may have become used to a sense of autonomy in most aspects of your life, so the experience of being constantly controlled is a distant memory. You have many responsibilities, but these are often connected to choices you make. To help you imagine how it feels to be in a heavily controlling environment, here is an analogy that you might relate to more readily:

Imagine that you are driving a car on a city street, with a brand new global positioning system (GPS). As usual, there are speed limits, signs, and painted lines to guide you. The road is a very structured environment, but you are still "in the driver's seat," so to speak.

You need some feedback to help you get where you are going, so you switch on your brand new GPS. To your surprise, the navigation system has some strong opinions about where you should go, and how to get there. You speed up to keep up with the other traffic on the road, and the GPS says: "No, you're going too fast. Slow down. That's better. I'll tell you when you can speed up again."

You take a turn to avoid some construction, and the GPS pipes up again: "Why did you take this road? I could have shown you a better way. There are at least three other faster routes."

You might still reach your destination, but not without thinking seriously about replacing the GPS (assuming it has not already been flung out the window). The task of driving a car is the same, but the experience becomes much more frustrating because of the controlling quality of the input.

We have examined the importance of choice and autonomy earlier in this section, but what about the students who would rather choose to do nothing at all, because any choice offered by an adult in authority seems somehow offensive to them? For an experienced teacher, this refusal can quickly sabotage plans, because setting up contingencies (in other words, "You do this, I give you that") is a very common strategy introduced in an effort to "motivate" students.

When a student refuses to pick a work task or select a preferred activity when offered a choice, this can really throw experienced teachers for a loop. (If you have met one of these students, you will recognize this pattern instantly. If you have not yet encountered this dilemma, count yourself lucky and keep reading!)

Some students diagnosed with ODD do struggle, even with teachers who have an autonomy-supporting style. Here are some possible reasons why:

- *Return to the familiarity of the power struggle:* Students who have spent most of their time in a controlling environment often develop skills that are specialized to cope and push back against outside pressure. They become experts in tolerating disapproval, ignoring feedback, recruiting peers, finding creative alternatives to the task at hand, and resisting outside influence. In an autonomy-supporting environment, the student must make use of a whole different skill set. The tactics of counter-control are not needed. Instead, the student must coordinate with others, express their values, and execute their plan with the help of the teacher. If the student cannot see when to make that switch, or is missing some of the skills required to thrive in an autonomy-supporting environment, then some counter-control-type behavior might be expected.
- *Sensitivity to perceived loss:* Choice can be particularly challenging for students who struggle with anxiety. Saying "yes" to one thing means saying "no" to (and potentially missing out on) any number of opportunities. Students with this type of "fear of missing out" may delay the choice until it is too late, or reject the whole task as a way of avoiding a choice that feels impossible.
- *Anxiety and perfectionism:* When students are offered the chance to choose their own direction and goals, they may hesitate out of fear that they will not make the correct choice, or delay getting started just because the result could be imperfect.
- *Paying a high price for choice:* When students are offered a choice in the context of a "reward" for a difficult task, over and over again, they may come to associate the choice with the demand (and control) that follows it. When a student's choice turns into the first step in a series of unpleasant tasks, they are forced to pay a heavy price each time a choice is offered. The student may then decide not to choose at all, knowing that their selection will be withheld and used as a "carrot" to motivate them to perform a task of the teacher's choosing.

As you can see, most of this reluctance is based on anxiety and suspicion, not "opposition" and "defiance." For students who are very sensitive to stress and for students who have a long history of struggle with adults, their classroom engagement will improve as their sense of safety and trust with you grows.

CONTROL AND THE COERCIVE CYCLE

Children diagnosed with ODD are sometimes presumed to love conflict for its own sake. While some children may naturally enjoy taking risks, finding enjoyment in the excitement of a conflict and the power they can wield, this is not the only reason why some children find themselves in conflict with adults over and over again.

In the previous section, you examined classroom dynamics through the lens of control. Teachers, like parents and politicians, are expected to use pressure to manage and shape classroom behavior. This type of control can be seen almost anywhere in everyday life. We take for granted that a police officer can issue demands to citizens when they see fit, and use threats and an escalating series of painful consequences to achieve compliance. Judges can set fines or prison sentences for people who refuse to follow directives based in law. Lenders can charge interest fees for late payments, or threaten to repossess assets. Like a referee blowing the whistle and giving a penalty to a player, parents withdraw privileges and schools give detentions in response to undesirable behavior.

When increasingly unpleasant consequences or hurtful tactics are used as a strategy to "win" in a situation, this is known as *coercion*. In a coercive situation, the message is: "Do what I want, or else." Coercion can take the form of a threat to gain compliance, or a punishment in response to defiance, in the hope that the misbehavior will not be repeated.

Coercion and patterns of escalation

Coercion usually begins with a mild response that becomes harsher or more intense if it is not successful. Unfortunately, if the mild response is not very effective, it tends to be dropped in favor of whatever gets the best result. You may have noticed this pattern with parents who complain that they must yell "all the time" because their polite requests are ignored, or when managers at a company introduce strict consequences to "crack down" on those who have been ignoring the gentle requests to comply. In other words, coercive tactics tend to get "shaped" over time, often becoming more severe.

The process of "shaping" (as the term is used in the field of behavior science) works a bit like the process of natural selection in evolution. That is, shaping:

- Often happens unintentionally
- Involves small, repeated changes over time
- Leads to changes that offer an advantage.

People are naturally prone to do what works best, so even a well-intentioned person can find themselves applying excessive pressure.

For instance, imagine that you have a door in your home that tends to stick when the weather is wet. On a rainy day, when you turn the doorknob gently and push, not much happens. When you first noticed this resistance, you tried jiggling the handle, checking the lock, and inspecting the hinges. After all, you are not a carpenter, so you don't have the tools to really deal with the effect of the humidity on the wood. What do you do? You might avoid using that door altogether, but often this is not possible, so you must find a way through. When your gentle fiddling with the doorknob didn't work, you leaned on the door with your shoulder, and it popped open. Your subtle problem-solving was largely unsuccessful, but brute force yielded instant results.

Since people tend to do what "works," your behavior might change in the days following this first shoulder tackle. Eventually, you've repeated this strategy so many times that when you approach this door, you grasp the doorknob and immediately lean on the door until it pops open, not bothering to try a gentler approach. You find yourself bursting through the door even when the weather is dry, because that's just what you've grown used to.

In other words, your technique for opening this sticky door changed because:

- Previous, less forceful attempts were unsuccessful
- Pressure on the door is the most reliable way to open it
- Repetition has created a habit that you don't think much about anymore.

In the same way, aggressive and disruptive behavior can develop as a habitual solution to a problem, especially when earlier, less forceful efforts have been unsuccessful, or when the tools to find a gentle solution are lacking.

Coercive cycles between children and adults

Most teachers have seen the process of shaping interacting with rule-breaking in their own classrooms, even in subtle ways. For example, if the teacher requires students to raise their hand before speaking, students can become impatient and shout out answers. "Shouting out" is a more forceful approach, but it stands a chance of successfully grabbing the teacher's attention. If the teacher responds to it, the disruption is more effective than waiting one's turn, so this tactic can be shaped into a hard habit to break. Remember: the goal of this behavior isn't explicitly to be rebellious, to annoy the teacher, or to prove a point. It's just an example of how rule-breaking can persist and escalate when it serves a purpose.

Let us bear this in mind as we look at how disruptive behavior can spark a power struggle. To illustrate this process in a general way:

1. A person encounters a problem, and gentle attempts to appeal for help or solve the problem cooperatively are unsuccessful.
2. The person is discouraged by these unsuccessful attempts.
3. The person lacks the skills or means to find other solutions.
4. A harsher response gets the desired reaction from the other people in the situation.
5. Harsh responses become the norm; gentle responses are discarded as unhelpful.
6. Harsh responses may increase the resistance from other people and escalate the situation, which starts the cycle all over again.

In the classroom, teachers do sometimes resort to coercion as a controlling tactic. Presumably, the goal is not to intimidate students but to maintain structure and good order. When a deliberate coercive strategy works as intended, the person in authority gives the threat, and the person with less power obeys.

Oppositional defiant disorder and coercive family processes

Some research on the topic of antisocial behavior suggests that coercion can be learned within the context of parent–child interactions. The pattern follows the same path as above:

1. A parent approaches the child with a polite request.
2. The child loudly refuses.
3. The parent retreats, discouraged, not sure what else to do.
4. The parent tries again, presenting the request in harsher terms, perhaps applying pressure by threatening to remove privileges.
5. If the high-pressure tactic is successful, then the parent is likely to repeat it, modeling coercive behavior for the child.
6. If the child responds with an even more forceful protest, such as aggression, property destruction, or threats of their own, the parent retreats, and the child is able to escape the demand with the use of antisocial behavior.

This cycle is certainly present in some family dynamics, and there is an undeniable logic to the way parents and children respond to pressure from one another. However, not all antisocial behavior can be assigned such a clear-cut motive (Coyne & Cairns 2016).

Counter-control and coercive cycles

"Give 'em an inch and they'll take a mile." This idiom illustrates the commonly held belief that if you were to make a small concession, you risk letting someone take advantage of you. In this case, even the threat of coercion would be enough to justify a rigid approach. Some adults act accordingly, assuming that children who misbehave are deliberately testing or undermining adult authority. These adults fear that if they tolerate or fail to deal with misbehavior, their ability to control the classroom will be jeopardized.

In truth, the reasons for challenging behavior in the classroom are rarely that simple. In some cases, ruling with an iron fist can make disruptive behavior even more likely, when students:

- Push back against any and all demands (this type of behavior is sometimes called "counter-control")
- Seek out a way to get their needs met, usually when other types of requests have failed
- Experience stress and helplessness and act out in emotional ways.

As you can see, when student misbehavior is interpreted as a challenge, teachers tend to respond by taking even more "disciplinary" action. This does not address the actual reason for the disruption, but works to highlight who is "in control" and who is expected to follow.

The problem with punishment

As you have read, the "manage-and-discipline" model of behavior depends on maintaining a system of incentives and disincentives. School policies often include a list of "dos and don'ts" that are enforced by an escalating series of undesirable consequences. These consequences vary from school to school, but common disciplinary techniques include:

- Public correction
- Warning
- Public shaming
- Name on the board
- Clip chart
- Parent feedback
- In-school suspension
- At-home suspension
- Expulsion
- Juvenile detention or prison.

The purpose of a punishment is ostensibly to "make 'em feel worse so they'll do better." Although corporal punishment (such as caning or smacking with a ruler) is banned in many school districts, the most common school response to repeated misbehavior is often some kind of punitive reaction. This system is familiar to us because a punishment-based response is frequently used in most public institutions. As adults, we expect others to react this way and we regulate our behavior in public with the expectation that our mistakes will be punished. We could be asked to leave the store, issued a citation and a ticket, handed a fine, or have our property seized or freedom restricted. In sports games, athletes who cheat are given penalties and time off the field.

This model is simple and familiar. It is supported by a common desire for justice, protection, and deterrence. You will hear people express these sentiments in support of punishment in many ways:

He has to understand that it's not acceptable.
It's not fair to the other students. She can't be allowed to get away with it.
There has to be some kind of consequence, otherwise how will they learn?
We have to prepare them for the real world.
Spare the rod and spoil the child.

Although the "manage-and-discipline" approach is culturally familiar and accepted, research shows that the efficacy of punishment is quite limited (Elbla 2012). Not only that: a punishment procedure can have many undesirable side effects.

Unfortunately, it is often difficult to separate opinion from fact where punishment is concerned. If an administrator, teacher, or parent holds positive opinions about punishment, it may be difficult for them to accept the following:

- Punishment does not teach new behaviors.
- Punishment does not deter if the behavior is not planned.
- Punishment does not deter if the goal of the behavior is urgent, reactive, stress-based, or meets a need.
- Punishment does not deter if it can be escaped.
- Punishment does not deter if it can be tolerated.
- Punishment can isolate students from their peers.
- Punishment can worsen anxiety and depression.
- Punishment does not deter if a student is less sensitive to it.
- Use of punishment can be mistaken for revenge or vindictiveness.
- Use of punishment by an adult can model the use of coercion for the student.

Essentially, punishment is a tool that is used to control and coerce. It undermines the effectiveness of the collaborative and autonomy-supporting techniques laid out in this book.

The word "discipline" has become synonymous in English usage with the word "punishment," but the Latin root of the word meant "teaching and instruction," or "to impose order upon." When you find yourself turning to methods of punishment for behavior management, or if you are under pressure from parents or administrators to dole out some kind of sentence, you can come back to the word "discipline" and ask yourself "What kind of learning experience can I create here?"

SUMMARY

What makes students listen to their teachers and obey the rules? In many schools, teachers offer rewards like gold stars, fun activities, or good grades to students who cooperate with the rules. If students do not follow the rules, teachers might send them to the principal's office, get angry with them in front of the class, or give them extra work to do. Many students choose to follow the rules to avoid punishment or to earn a reward. If the student continues to break school rules instead, they might get punished with stricter penalties.

You can use rewards and punishments to help you keep control of a class, but it does not work for every student. If your student is not interested in your rewards and can tolerate punishments, you do not have any way to control that student. Students diagnosed with oppositional defiant disorder (ODD) know how to resist when someone tries to control them.

If your student has been hurt or neglected by someone who tried to control them, they might try to avoid both rewards and punishments. Even prizes and good grades can make them feel like they are accepting your control.

Most people do not like to be controlled by others. It feels good to make choices. If you have choices, you can do what is important to you. You can do things in your own way. Even painful experiences are easier to handle when you are making a choice.

Adults often have control, but children do not. Your students probably get frustrated when they are under someone else's control, just like you do.

Students feel controlled when their teachers:

- Do not listen to their perspective
- Try to change what they think
- Pressure them until they obey.

If you want your students to cooperate with you, but you do not want to use control, you can attempt to create an "autonomy-supporting" classroom. If you want to be an autonomy-supporting teacher, you must do three important things:

- Listen to your students and invite them to give feedback.
- Help your students to understand why their cooperation is important.
- Give your students meaningful choices.

Teachers sometimes use warnings and punishments to get control in the classroom. When you punish or remove privileges from students who do not follow instructions, this is called "coercion." Students can use this strategy too. If your student punishes, avoids, or threatens you when you try to tell them what to do, this is called "counter-control."

If you use a gentle strategy, and it works, you will probably keep using it. If a gentle strategy doesn't work, you may try other strategies, including punishment. If students try to avoid the harsh strategies, or if they use a counter-control technique, you are back at the beginning, without a useful strategy. When one person uses a harsh strategy to get control, and the other person responds by trying even harder to escape, this is called a "coercive cycle."

Unfortunately, punishment can make your classroom problem worse. Punishment does not teach new behaviors. Students who are punished often become more anxious and depressed. Punishment does not always stop your student from misbehaving, especially when they are acting impulsively or in distress.

CHAPTER 6

LEADERSHIP WITHOUT COERCION

When you find yourself teaching a child diagnosed with ODD, you might be challenged to answer new kinds of questions from your student, such as:

Why should I?
Are you gonna make me?
Or what?

Although it may be extremely impolite for a child to confront an adult with this kind of blunt questioning, these questions are essentially worth asking. In fact, most people ask themselves the same kinds of questions when pressured to do something they don't want to do.

For an adult in a position of authority, the traditional answers to the question "Why should I?" may vary:

Because I asked you to.
Because all the other students are already finished.
Because if you don't, I'm sending you to the principal's office.
Because it's part of your education and it's good for you.

WORKING WITH YOUR STUDENTS, NOT AGAINST THEM

To be able to lead without coercion, you will need to step back from the "the carrot and the stick" as the basis of your classroom management strategy. In this section, you are invited to think deeply about what will take its place. Current research on motivation and child development suggests that students can thrive without pressure and coercion if they have two very powerful things:

- An autonomy-supporting environment
- An attuned relationship with a supportive adult.

Most teachers come into the classroom with a sincere desire to nurture their students' intrinsic motivation and to provide a warm and caring connection, but the demands of school curricula, tests, marking, permission slips, meetings, planning, and "classroom management" can quickly overwhelm. When a student introduces a disruption, such as a refusal or emotional outburst, there is a cost to the whole classroom. Lessons get delayed, and time and energy are spent trying to manage or minimize the problem behavior. There seems to be even less time available for "extras" like personal check-ins with students, creative problem-solving, or planning enjoyable activities. When there is a scarcity of time and resources, a controlling system can seem like the most efficient solution to managing problem behavior. Working on student relationships or digging into psychological questions may appear to be a luxury you cannot afford.

Autonomy and connection may seem to be subtle or complex at first glance, but in this section, you will find the *key components* of autonomy-supporting environments and attuned relationships, simplified and explained in practical steps, so you can focus your time and energy where it will make the biggest impact.

MOTIVATION WITHOUT COERCION

Even if you are not a psychology major, you have probably heard of the work of B. F. Skinner. His name is synonymous with *behaviorism*, a systematic approach for understanding the behavior of living things in terms of their learning histories. Skinner's experiments were mainly conducted using animals, and he demonstrated the vital importance of cues, timing, and consequences in the process of learning. Although some of his experiments seemed to be trivial or even absurd at face value (such as teaching pigeons to play nine-pin bowling), he understood that humans also respond to the opportunities in their environments. He speculated about how human cultures could be changed to allow people to live more satisfying and equitable lives. Skinner understood only too well that systems of control (using positive and/or aversive tactics) often have unwanted side effects, and he was not naive enough to suggest a universal system of behavior management for humankind, but he did write extensively on the need to "experiment... explore new ways of living" (1981, p.292).

Skinner's writing and research shed light on how behavior is changed when we encounter rewarding experiences. However, his work did not explain *why* certain human experiences are so rewarding, or how our thoughts and emotions influence these outcomes. Fortunately, in the decades that followed, researchers like Richard M. Ryan, Edward L. Deci, and many others, have taken up questions like this.

As a teacher, learning and motivation are at the heart of your practice. If you see that certain students are not responding well to the tools you have on hand, you will find some opportunity here to "experiment" and "explore," as Skinner suggested, to find new ways to capture motivation and inspire cooperation.

BEYOND "EXTRINSIC VERSUS INTRINSIC"

Using external pressures and incentives is sometimes referred to as "extrinsic motivation," and the limits of its effectiveness are clear. If teachers were required to dole out treats, praise, and points for every single behavior, they would quickly be overwhelmed by the demands of tracking and responding to students pushing in their chairs or lining up for recess. Students could refuse to cooperate without sufficiently valuable incentives, dental bills would skyrocket as candies flowed into the classroom currency, and little rewards like stickers would quickly lose their appeal. In other words, operant responding (see table) is an excellent model for training, but it does not fully capture the full breadth of the human experience.

Similarly, a system set up on self-interest alone does not offer the right conditions for a community of learners. It is difficult to imagine a classroom that would function with students only doing the activities they *felt like* doing, without feedback, suggestions, or encouragement from the teacher. People (including, and perhaps especially, children) often make choices that act against their own best interests, and some structure and influence from an outside source is necessary to guide a group of individuals to accomplish a common goal.

In a group, there are many expectations that will challenge your students and push them outside their comfort zone, so you are working to manage motivation all the time. Most importantly, you are:

- Boosting motivation for tasks that will help students meet their full academic potential and overall wellbeing
- Minimizing motivation for behaviors that are dangerous or harmful, such as aggression, protest, teasing, or disruption.

A CLOSER LOOK AT REWARDS, INCENTIVES, AND VALUES

In preparation for a deeper dive into motivation at school, let us review a few facts about what makes an experience rewarding. There are many different ways of understanding rewards, but we don't need to study the finer points of the ventromedial prefrontal cortex or compare humanist psychology against operant conditioning to discuss how to be a really effective teacher. We will discuss rewards in the broadest terms possible, so we can incorporate the findings of many different scientific fields. Essentially, for the purposes of this book, the term "reward" is used to describe "something that makes a behavior more likely to occur." Hopefully, this definition will be both simple and practical.

A given behavior is more likely to occur when it meets an important need or leads to a reward. The power of this motivation will change depending on other factors, such as life experiences, maturity, illness, and other situational cues.

Type of need	Example
Basic biological drives (Skinner 1984)	We tend to experience pleasure when we attend to those needs, and we tend to feel uncomfortable when those needs are not met. We make time to eat, drink, and rest each day, no matter what else is happening.
Basic social needs (Jones *et al.* 2011)	We all have a powerful need for safety, belonging, and attachment.

Physiological state (Carter & Driscoll 2007)	An emotional or hormonal change, such as depression, fear, infatuation, curiosity, anger, or fatigue, influences the amount of effort that behavior requires, or the amount of pleasure or pain that we might experience.
Operant conditioning (Mazur 1991)	We often persist if the same behavior has led to an immediately rewarding result, such as pleasure or relief, or something that has been associated with an immediate rewarding result, such as money. When the result is delayed or mildly pleasant, the effect is reduced.
Chains of behaviors (Logan & Spanier 1970)	We also tend to repeat a series of steps if it triggers another event and this eventually leads to a pleasant outcome.
Rule-governed behavior (Catania, Shimoff, & Matthews 1989)	Our thoughts and beliefs influence our expectations, so we take action even when we have no prior experience or there is a long delay between behavior and beneficial outcome (such as social approval or material gain).
Values (Reilly *et al.* 2019)	We tend to find hard things easier when they align with individual, closely held values or beliefs about what is important and meaningful in life.

In school, there may be no immediate pay-off for writing an essay or standing in line. Quite a few students would willingly follow the school rules to avoid an unpleasant telling-off from the teacher, so obedience is somewhat rewarding as far as it helps them "stay out of trouble." However, this only supports basic compliance in terms of school expectations. To motivate a student to work harder and go beyond the minimum standard, some other goal or value is necessary. Typically, students can expect some reward or benefit for participating in school and following teacher expectations.

Examples of rewards and incentives offered, from very immediate to very delayed

- *Daily:* Verbal praise from the teacher, posting work on the wall, time to relax after work is completed, privileges
- *Weekly:* Assignments handed back with grades, classroom contests
- *Term:* End-of-term report cards
- *Year:* Yearly reports, promotion to next grade
- *Extended:* Graduation, access to college or university, scholarships.

There are different types of motivation involved in each of these promises. Operant conditioning helps to explain why getting immediate feedback or relief from discomfort is so effective. As the length of time between the behavior and the promised reward increases, the effectiveness of the promised reward depends on whether the student takes on thoughts, beliefs, and values that sustain the importance of the reward.

Some teachers add extra incentives into the classroom environment, such as sticker charts to display each student's achievements, or accumulated rewards for group cooperation (such as a pizza party if the class earns the required number of points). Unfortunately, there are limits to what this kind of reward can achieve. In order to increase student engagement and reduce problem behavior, the value of the reward must be powerful enough to compensate for the effort of compliance. If breaking the rules or avoiding the task could potentially lead to a bigger "pay-off," the reward loses its appeal. If the student is lacking the skills to reliably perform the required action, the reward cannot be achieved at all.

Rewards can also backfire in unpleasant ways:

- Some students have an anxious reaction to planned incentives, worried about a possible loss instead of feeling excited about the potential gain.
- Offering rewards for a task that a student already enjoys can dampen their existing enthusiasm if the reward is added and then discontinued.
- Students may try to find other ways to access the reward (e.g., cheating, stealing, whining, threatening, pressuring other students to do it for them).
- Students may become upset or angry if there is disagreement as to whether the reward has been earned.
- If a group member does not perform as expected, peers may lash out in frustration.
- Students may refuse to perform in exchange for "rewards" if they perceive it to be part of a controlling system.
- Students may opt to perform only when rewards are offered, and refuse other tasks.

Supporting values and long-term goals

A short-term reward for every aspect of compliance is unfeasible and frankly unnecessary, but ideally, students will agree to make an effort in the short term in exchange for some longer-term pay-off. If a student can bear these long-term rewards in mind, they will be prepared to persevere and grind even when the demands are difficult. The ability to delay gratification tends to develop as students age and mature, but younger or more impulsive students may need some help to go from one task to the next.

Immediacy is part of what makes short-term rewards so powerful. When delivery of a reward is delayed, the perceived value of the reward dwindles too. This phenomenon is called "delay discounting", and has been well researched in many different populations. One of the first demonstrations of this is the often-repeated marshmallow test (Mischel & Ebbesen 1970). Dr Mischel's team began testing groups of very young children to see if they would be willing to resist a treat placed in front of them while the experimenter left the room. In exchange, the researchers promised that after the wait was over and the experimenter returned, the children would be able to consume not only the first treat, but another one as well.

As Dr Mischel and his team repeated the experiment with slight variations, they found that while some children would inevitably opt to eat the treat right away (and give up the promise of another), the children were able to hold out longer under certain specific conditions.

If you keep these conditions in mind, you may be able to set up your classroom so that your students can better resist short-term gratification in favor of important longer-term goals.

1. Momentum and structure help students stay on target

Dr Mischel found that children were more willing to wait in exchange for a second treat when they were instructed to think about something fun (as opposed to thinking about eating the treat), or when they were given an object to play with as they waited. Children in the experiment found it hard to resist temptation when there was nothing else to occupy them. Similarly, classroom rules are especially hard to enforce in periods of "down time" when students are at loose ends.

Here are some strategies to help you if unstructured periods are getting turbulent in your classroom:

- Smooth, speedy transitions from one activity to another
- Clear instructions to help students start a task
- Activities to keep students occupied after they finish a task
- Hints and help to redirect students when they get stuck.

2. Students are more willing to delay gratification for a teacher who is reliable

Children in the experiment were less likely to succumb to short-term gratification when they had reason to trust that the experimenter would fulfill their promise. If the experimenter had previously failed to deliver on a promise, the children were less likely to wait. Here are some strategies to help you build trust so that students will:

- Create predictable daily routines
- Build credibility by fulfilling small promises before making bigger promises
- Confirm classroom rules and expectations in writing.

3. Information about the length of the wait helps support delayed gratification

When children were not given information about when the experimenter would return, they were more likely to end the experiment early and simply eat the first treat. Here are some strategies to help your students pace themselves and increase their persistence:

- Visual schedules
- Time Timer
- Allow students to choose their own intervals
- Demonstrate the "Pomodoro" technique (alternating between scheduled intervals of work and breaks) (see Cirillo 2006).

Values

Each student comes to your class with their own set of values and ideas about what makes life meaningful. Values can come from a student's personal identity and also from their community. Fortunately, classroom activities can be infused with many different values, so you can offer your students the opportunity to make that connection.

Every value comes with a set of corresponding behaviors. These often involve some kind of exchange or effort. For example, if you value punctuality, you will leave the house in plenty of time to ensure that you are not late. If you value generosity, you might bring an extra coffee with you to give away at school. Value-driven behaviors do not have an immediate payback, and they may never result in a tangible gain, but the behavior is itself imbued with importance and meaning.

As you praise your students, keep their values in mind. Praise communicates more than just social approval. In fact, the power of your praise can be boosted if it matches the values of the student. What would your students say if you asked them to choose some words that best describe what is important to them?

It's important to me to be...		
Sincere	Persistent	Secure
Curious	Brave	Connected
Creative	Serious	Healthy
Considerate	Joyful	Honest
Encouraging	Helpful	Independent
Wise	Strong	Fair

When you discuss values with your students, be sure to emphasize the individual quality of values. Everyone is free to choose the values that bring meaning and importance to their lives.

As you can see, when we focus on the student's experience (and not on the consequences of their behavior), we can add rich satisfaction and meaning to daily tasks without as many artificial pressures. If you take away anything from this chapter, let it be this:

Motivation does not come from inside the student.
Motivation is always in flux, always responding to changes in the environment.
Motivation is influenced by beliefs and experiences, but it can always be nurtured.

THREE MOTIVATION BOOSTERS YOU CAN USE THROUGHOUT THE DAY

As you might guess by the word "defiant," students diagnosed with ODD often seem unmotivated and unwilling to say "yes" when asked to perform. Maximizing motivation is a wise strategy when working with these students.

To answer the question of what motivates people (apart from immediate gain), Edward Deci, Richard Ryan, and others set up experiments and compared groups of people working under different conditions. These studies focused on the contrast between behavior when it is being directly managed or influenced by incentives and threats, and behavior that is self-directed. For example, they noted the paradoxical effect of extrinsic reinforcers on certain types of activities. In one well-known experiment (Deci, Koestner, & Ryan 1999), they showed that, in some cases, people would spend less time on a preferred activity after they had received a reward for it. In other words, they studied what they called *intrinsic motivation*, with and without the presence of rewards.

Deci and Ryan (2004) also found that the groups who were most interested, engaged, and motivated had a few conditions in common. They concluded that these conditions were gratifying because they must be satisfying an important psychological need. They described these needs as:

- *Autonomy:* the freedom to make meaningful choices.
- *Relatedness:* a sense of connection and belonging.
- *Competence:* the opportunity to improve or progress.

Aside from the psychological needs described by Deci and Ryan, it is important to note here that classroom activities can certainly be enjoyable for their own sake. Play, exploration, curiosity, joy, and humor are naturally rewarding. Classroom activities can be made more intrinsically motivating when they involve student interests. Many excellent books have been written on how to make the classroom environment fun and engaging, but even when a school task is not suited to the taste of your students, you can still infuse it with more value when you consider Deci and Ryan's proposed psychological needs. The next time you sense that an activity is something to "just get through" because it's on the curriculum, consider how to add elements of *autonomy*, *relatedness*, and *competence* to the learning experience.

Students who are unmotivated or resistant are often missing these three experiences. They have not felt free and have had painful experiences with systems of control. They are anxious to avoid situations that don't offer a sense of competence. They believe their interests are separate from those of the group, so they don't feel related. They are not truly "opposed" to their role as a student or "defiant" of the school rules. Rather, they often opt out when they reach a state of frustration and disconnection.

Freedom to make meaningful choices

The term *autonomy* has been mentioned earlier in this book, as an alternative to "control." Autonomy refers to the ability to choose experiences that are interesting and important, without pressure from anyone else. The freedom to choose one's own path seems to add enjoyment and purpose to many different activities.

Examples from everyday life:

- Shopping
- Making art

- Hobbies
- Travelling.

Examples in the classroom:

- Personal storytelling
- Choice of format
- Choice of topics

- Choice of activities
- Selecting books to read.

However, as it turns out, pure freedom is not a source of complete happiness (if it were, parents would never hear their children complain of boredom on a Saturday afternoon). Alongside autonomy, two other factors seem to help to make an experience valuable and satisfying: the ability to grow and excel, and belonging and feeling safe in a group.

The ability to grow and excel

Competence, a sense of growth and "leveling up," is a natural reward that sustains motivation even under difficult circumstances.

Examples from everyday life:

- High scores in video games
- Promotions at work
- Personal fitness goals.

Examples in the classroom:

- Fluency
- Competition
- Self-assessment.

Belonging and feeling safe in a group

Relatedness, a sense of connection to others and a belonging in the group, also adds value to an experience (Cabello & Terrell 1994).

Examples from everyday life:

- Team sports
- Religious communities

- Genealogy and family reunions
- Local traditions.

Examples in the classroom:

- School spirit
- Classroom traditions
- Conflict negotiation
- Inclusive and anti-racist themes

- Classroom pride
- Shared values, class motto
- Group activities.

SUMMARY

You should think carefully about what motivates your student. Every student wants to know: "Why should I do this?" If you try to control your students' behavior with rewards and punishments, you will be effective only part of the time. Students will ignore rewards and punishments if they are motivated for their own reasons, or if they want to avoid control. Your students' natural motivation is always changing, but if you understand it, you can capture it more often.

Here are some ways to increase your students' natural motivation:

- Listen to your students and give them meaningful choices.
- Make sure your students see and celebrate their own progress.
- Help each student feel safety and belonging in the classroom.
- Share with your students why the activity is good for them.
- Talk to your students about what they find meaningful, so you can connect activities to their values.
- Stay organized to avoid long waits and confusion.
- Keep your promises so your students will trust you.
- Use visuals and timers to let your students know what is coming next.

CHAPTER 7

BUILDING TRUST AND CONNECTION

To put it simply, any system that is not built on control and coercion must be built on trust instead. Trust is a hard concept to define. It's about more than being reliable or responsible. In the context of relationships, the definition developed by John Gottman is a useful one (2011): when you trust someone, you will behave as if they have your best interests at heart. You will behave as if nothing will be done at your expense.

Without trust, we have to look out and make sure that other people don't interfere with our needs and desires. In the classroom, a student who lacks trust must carefully weigh each new demand the teacher places:

Is this going to help me?
Will this be fun?
Am I going to be able to do this?
Is this fair?
Is this worth my time and energy?
Is this going to cost me?

Although you may do your best to connect with each of your students, there are various reasons why these efforts may fall short at first:

- The student may have a painful history with adults in authority (Gregory & Weinstein 2008).
- You and your students may find yourself struggling to connect due to a difference in personality, life experience, and preferences.
- If you have clashed with this student, it may be hard to overcome grudges and mistrust.
- You may struggle with stereotypes and prejudice related to age, faith practices, gender, race, socioeconomic status, or affiliation.
- Cultural differences can lead to misunderstandings and missed opportunities for communication.

Without trust, you may be constantly challenged, and asked to justify the need for the instructions you give. However, in a trusting relationship, what's good for one person is probably good for the other too. As a teacher managing a large group of children, you are still tasked with setting up learning opportunities and providing structure, clear expectations, and directions. With trust, it's safe for the student to cooperate with you. Even without a carrot or a stick, your student is willing to go along with your instructions.

As you have read, students diagnosed with ODD often come to the classroom discouraged, defensive, and demoralized after repeated conflicts and power struggles. You can create a rich and meaningful learning environment in the classroom and plan intriguing lessons, but learning must also happen within the context of safe, connected relationships.

Have you ever noticed that some teachers just have a "way" with difficult students? Perhaps you are one of those teachers who gets called to negotiate stand-offs and console tearful students. It's hard to explain exactly what makes a teacher approachable. Even if you have the knack, it is difficult to articulate how it works. Fortunately, some researchers have taken on the challenge of breaking this down, and, as it turns out, you do not have to have much in common with your student to build rapport. You do not need to hand out candy or persuade a student to "like" you in order to build a positive foundation for a relationship. To build rapport, research suggests you must do three things:

- *Be warm:* Highlight the value of connectedness and belonging. Share enthusiasm and joy.
- *Be interested:* Notice small changes in your student, paying attention to what interests them.
- *Be responsive:* Be ready to respond to small changes in your student's behavior.

These three practices, when done consistently and with sensitivity, will create the conditions necessary for a trusting relationship, so that students are less defensive, less anxious, and more willing to connect with you. As you engage with your student and you demonstrate acceptance, they will become more open to influence and more willing to share important thoughts and ideas with you. Most importantly, your student will get the message that you understand their goals and needs, and will act with their best interests at heart.

As a teacher, you have your own personal style of social communication, and most of your training was probably more concerned with pedagogy than psychology. The building blocks of rapport-building may not have been part of your coursework, but these practices have been used by social workers and therapists to create an avenue toward trust. If you have tried to connect with your students but something seems to be missing, you can use this section to explore each aspect of rapport-building in your practice.

Rapport-building is never a straightforward process, and there will be plenty of bumps along the way. It is vitally important for you to remember what you have learned about stress responses, so you can observe small changes in your students' body language as you offer opportunities to connect. If you see signs of distress when you approach, you can pause to reevaluate.

On good days, you may see a bit of mutual understanding start to grow, but with some students, the first sparks of connection seem to be quickly extinguished when their mood changes, or when you place a demand that does not agree with them. If you are continually struggling with this student to try to keep them on task, interrupting aggressive outbursts, and denying them access to preferred activities, you may find that there's very little room left in the day left for interactions that include positivity, coordination, and attention. However, once you have run into a conflict or misunderstanding, you will go through a process of repair. Your willingness to stay connected with your student, even through difficult situations, can strengthen the bond of trust between you.

BE WARM

Warmth, or positivity, is more than just cheerfulness, conditional praise, or approval. In behavioral terms, warmth can be understood as a kind of "noncontingent reinforcement." Nothing is required to earn it; it is just freely available. Warmth requires the willingness to accept your student with grace and understanding on both good days and bad, and to extend kindness in moments of disagreement.

When you cultivate positivity in the classroom, you spend more time pointing out strengths than weaknesses, and students learn that they are valued for who they are, not just for the work they turn in. Warmth and positivity are important to maintain even in moments of conflict. Your facial expression, your choice of language, and your nonverbal communication can all help to send the message: *we are on the same team. I'm here for you.*

When warmth is missing, it's hard to build an alliance with a student who has come into the classroom with their own goals. Without positivity, your priorities and the student's priorities are probably at odds with each other. Without positivity, your calm tone of voice could be interpreted as detached, icy, or hostile. If your only communication is to give instructions and corrections, your students will learn that when you walk into the room, hard work is sure to follow. Some leaders do manage to function this way, but their focus is on performance and competition.

Here are some practical ways to be warm in the classroom:

- A sincere and friendly greeting is a good start. Your expression and tone of voice should send the message: "It's good to see you. I'm glad you're here."
- Every day, you can find an opportunity to notice some improvement or effort.
- Resist jumping to conclusions. Try to give the benefit of the doubt, and let your students know that you assume the best, not the worst.

- Introduce students to things you find personally uplifting and encouraging. Invite them to share their own.
- Be human. Admit mistakes, laugh at yourself, and be honest when you are not sure.
- Make room for activities that allow students to express their thoughts and priorities.
- Find out what your students value, and let them know you care about their priorities.

Some attempts at positivity do go awry. If you do offer compliments, be sure that they are culturally appropriate, not so over-the-top that they sound insincere, or so generic that they don't seem to refer to anything in particular. If you praise, keep it separate from comments that include constructive criticism, and praise students for their genuine effort, not just for excellent outcomes.

BE INTERESTED

Attention is a simple idea to understand. It is like a light that shines wherever you look. When you bring your student into focus, notice what they are doing, or make an effort to send a message to them, this is attention.

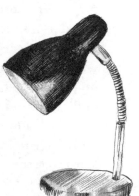

All of us need attention at times. We are social creatures, and when we are acknowledged, we are reminded that we matter. In a classroom, your attention can be particularly valuable because so many different events are competing for your attention at any given moment.

Not all attention is positive, of course. Teachers and parents are often advised to spend more time noticing appropriate behavior, and to "catch 'em being good" because it's so much easier to pay attention when something unexpected or disruptive happens. Compliance rarely attracts as much attention as trouble.

Not all students welcome attention from a teacher, of course. If the student has a long learning history involving correction and punishment from teachers, they may wish to avoid your attention altogether. Attention can even be frightening or threatening, if they feel unsure or "singled out." This is an area where cultural competence is extremely important. Some students may welcome a joke or a smile, while others would be uncomfortable with direct eye contact. A private chat after class is a kind of attention that some students would happily engage in, while others would rather sink through the floor.

Your students will react differently to your attention based on your gender, your age, your cultural background, and perhaps even your life experience. Learn as much as you can about how attention is given in their cultural background, so you can choose your body language and word choice accordingly.

Strange as it may seem, it comes down to this: *pay attention to what happens when you pay attention.* Without attention, a student may feel as if they are just part of the crowd, "going along to get along." Without attention, there is no sense of togetherness, no assurance that your priorities are the same. Consequently, it becomes hard for the student to follow your instructions without questioning how it will benefit them.

Here are some practical ways to pay attention and notice each day:

- When you speak to your students, make sure you have the opportunity to address them at their own eye level every so often.
- If they are anxious or withdrawn, they may not be ready to have the spotlight shining on them directly, but you will often be able to work on an activity side by side.
- Paying attention to one another is important, but shared attention can be very powerful too. Notice what your students look at. Look at those things together.
- Make sure to say their name to invite and to share with them, not just to correct them.
- Scan the room, but challenge yourself to spend a few moments watching one student at a time, if you can.
- Put students at ease with sensory activities and fidgets they can manipulate as you converse, so your attention can move back and forth.
- If your student is uncomfortable with conversation or if they are nonverbal, physical activities can be an excellent opportunity to share attention and coordinate. Even if you are just kicking a ball back and forth, or picking up and moving a table together, you are inviting them into your world.
- Maintain a sense of curiosity about your students. Even when their behavior is not what you were hoping for, you still can say to yourself "This is actually kind of fascinating!" instead of "Oh, how frustrating!"

BE RESPONSIVE

Responding is a subtle process of reacting to little changes in the other person's behavior. Drivers on the highway must coordinate with each other or else they will crash. Dancers imitate each other, move in opposition, and then come back together. Conversation partners take turns so they don't interrupt each other.

Whether you mean to or not, you and your students are responding to each other all the time. Teachers notice when students glance at the clock and hurry to finish their lessons. Students look around to see who else is willing to answer a question before raising a hand. When you deliver the lesson you have prepared, you are responding to their body language and pausing to answer their questions.

Coordination is also extremely important from a trauma-informed perspective, because your ability to detect little changes and body language can enable you to spot a trauma response before it escalates. You are moving around the classroom to keep an eye on some students whispering in the corner. In your one-on-one conversations with students, coordination happens as you take turns to speak, but your nonverbal communication is also coordinated. If your student leans away from you, you stand at a respectful distance. If they lower their voice, you speak more quietly too.

Not all classroom activities require coordination, of course. When you write an email, mark a test, or prepare a lesson, you might be keeping your student in mind, but there's no immediate back-and-forth.

If you try to interact but you are not aware of your partner's nonverbal signals or if you choose to ignore them, coordination does not occur. In that case, one partner dominates and the other has no influence. Nonverbal communication is dismissed, and important opportunities for connection are lost. For some students, being ignored or overlooked is a very painful experience, so your willingness to respond makes you a safer person to talk to.

- Notice your students' body language, and how it changes depending on where you stand or the tone of voice you use.
- People who are attuned tend to mirror each other's body language. If you see this happening, take it as a good sign!
- Active listening techniques help coordination by checking for understanding.
- Resist the urge to interrupt, and leave space in the conversation for your students to fill in.

SUMMARY

Your students need to be able to trust you. They need to know that you will make choices that are good for them. You can show your students that you are trustworthy by doing three important things:

- *Be warm:* Show your students that you notice their strengths. Appreciate your students for who they are. Accept their mistakes and keep working to connect with them.
- *Be attentive:* Each student in your class needs to know that they matter. Watch your students carefully so you can learn more about them.
- *Be responsive:* Be prepared to make a change if your approach is not working. You can change your pace, body language, words, or even your expectations. When you can be flexible, your students will feel safer.

CHAPTER 8

RESPONDING TO STUDENTS IN DISTRESS

Many students diagnosed with ODD struggle with emotional self-regulation and impulse control. Worse, these students generally express their emotions in a way that can be disruptive or offensive to others. Our understanding of emotional self-regulation in children is still developing, but it has come a long way. Not so long ago, children who expressed emotional sensitivity were subjected by a process of desensitization to "toughen them up." Parents were accused of "coddling" their children if they responded to cries of distress. Children were labeled "manipulative" if they expressed unhappiness or anger.

We now understand that children develop emotional self-regulation skills in the context of a safe, caring relationship.

Instead of relying on...	Adults can also support...
Ignoring or time-outs to stop challenging behavior	Secure and caring connections
Predictable consequences to teach cause-and-effect	Cognitive skills that help with problem-solving and self-control
Self-soothing and commands to "stop"	Physiological and neurological processes that control stress, fear, and recovery

NOTICING SIGNS OF STRESS

If you can be alert to early signs of distress, you will find it much easier to adjust and respond than if you are trying to contain a student having a full-blown meltdown. Here are some signs to look for.

When your student is experiencing the fight, flight, or freeze response, you will see some changes in their body language and behavior that indicate an increase in stress, anxiety, or post-traumatic stress symptoms. Typically, you will notice one primary stress response to begin with (fight, flight, or freeze), and if the situation escalates, they may communicate their distress with one of the other types of responses (e.g., fighting when an attempt to flee is blocked).

This is particularly important with students who have a history of trauma and neglect. Their autonomic nervous systems are easily hijacked, they will perceive a threat when no threat is present, and they will respond in unexpected ways (e.g., fight, flight, or freeze).

There are a few typical ways a stress response will present itself.

Fight

In the initial stages of a fight response, you may see changes such as:

- Raised shoulders
- Exhaling heavily
- Head down, looking from side to side
- Tightly curled hands.

As the fight response escalates, you might also notice:

- Raised voice
- Pacing around
- Glaring
- Stomping or hitting surfaces
- Emphatic gestures, such as pointing.

Note: A "fight" response does not always look hostile, but could be mistaken for hyper-arousal, including laughter and talking non-stop. Some students will initially try to distance themselves from a threat, so their response looks more like "flight."

Flight

At first, you may see changes in your student's behavior, such as:

- Shallow breathing
- Ducking down
- Stepping back or behind a piece of furniture
- Hugging an object close to the midsection of the body
- Quieter voice
- Looking down.

As the flight response escalates, you might see even more defensive body language, such as:

- Leaving the room
- Running away
- Shouting "Get away" or "Shut up"
- Throwing objects when people approach.

Freeze

People who experience the "freeze" response sometimes report a feeling of sleepiness and confusion when they experience a stress reaction. If a student is feeling "frozen," you might notice changes in their behavior, such as:

- Appearing withdrawn
- Refusing to speak
- Holding a rigid body posture
- Negative, dismissive statements
- Blank facial expression.

As the freeze response escalates, you might see changes such as:

- Covering their face
- Refusing to move in any direction
- Actually falling asleep.

SUPPORTING WITHOUT CONTROLLING

When you witness this behavior, you will probably notice your own stress levels start to increase. If it is safe to do so, take a moment to collect your resolve before you assess the situation and choose what priority you will focus on. In this section, you have a chance to consider your priorities proactively, so you are not improvising or responding in the heat of the moment.

In cultures where teachers are praised for "controlling" their classes, you may be tempted to jump into the fray and start giving instructions, asserting authority, issuing warnings, etc. If your students were behaving rationally in that moment, then your instructions and warnings would be useful information about how not to "get into trouble." However, for students who struggle with emotional regulation, logical reasoning gets discarded in favor of emotional expression. In fact, some students will escalate their challenging behavior when they are confronted with a cool, rational argument.

If you have the opportunity to attend training on nonviolent crisis prevention or intervention, this will be a worthwhile investment for you. Check with your administration to see what resources are available, or what protocols have been developed for helping students in crisis. If your school does not have a protocol, you will want to seek out training so you can develop your own, preferably one that is individualized for each student who needs it.

As you create your protocol, consider how to arrange your priorities in the right order, to maximize the effectiveness of each action you take. Here is one possible sequence:

1. Ensure physical *safety* for you, your student, and other classmates.
2. Communicate in a way that feels *kind* and safe for your student. If you use your

voice, moderate your tone and volume. Use words sparingly at first. Consider other ways of communication, such as nonverbal and written.

3. Listen with the intention of *understanding* your student's emotional state (even if the facts are in dispute).

4. Look for an emotional *de-escalation* before attempting to give orders or problem-solve with your student.

5. Offer choices and communicate *boundaries*.

SUMMARY

Many students diagnosed with oppositional defiant disorder (ODD) have emotional highs and lows. When your students are stressed and upset, they may not listen to your instructions. They may act loud, rude, or dangerous. If you get to know your students well, you might be able to see changes in their body language when they start to get upset. When you notice that your student is upset, you might want to focus on helping them to feel safe. When your student feels safe, they will find it easier to calm down. If a student is having problems with emotional outbursts, you should make a plan with your student and include other school staff so your student knows what to expect. Boundaries and rules are important, but if you try to discuss them with your student in the middle of an emotional outburst, you might make the situation worse.

THREE GIFTS YOU CAN GIVE YOURSELF AND SHARE WITH YOUR STUDENTS

From one teacher to another, my best advice is to bring three important gifts into the classroom with you:

- *Calm:* Self-regulation comes from the accumulation of habits, and these are built up over time. When you practice taking deep breaths, you may find it awkward at first, but as time goes on, it becomes a restorative and useful pause. Calm is more than just self-control. When you are in the habit of noticing and then letting go of anxious or self-critical thoughts, you can deal with them before they become overwhelming. When you are aware of the signs of stress in your body, you can take little moments of mindful relaxation before you are in a state of distress.

- *Confidence:* Inner confidence can also be understood as a kind of optimism. If you walk into the classroom knowing that you are not going to be measured, that you may stumble but you can learn from mistakes, and that you are worthy of kindness or respect, then the behavior of other people will have less of an impact on your wellbeing. When you trust in your own worth, you see the behavior of other people in a new way. It's not a judgment, an assessment, or an indictment of how capable you are as a teacher. When someone is disruptive or rude, you will remember everything that might have led up to that moment aside from your own input, such as a student's argument with a parent, a nasty text message, a difficult night's sleep, or a dull previous class: in other words, confidence helps you when you are tempted to take things personally.

- *Compassion:* Compassion can be defined as mercy, unearned. When you are prepared to be kind to students even when they are unkind, and you offer patience to students who are prickly with you, you are bringing compassion and grace into the classroom with you. The beauty of compassion is that it does not  demand an instant return. You are offering mercy for its own sake. Over time, grace can help to soften a grudge, and it acts as a powerful demonstration of self-control and kindness. Compassion can also help you overlook little irritations in the classroom that would otherwise distract or spiral into full-blown confrontations. Best of all, it can be completely unexpected, which is often a useful strategy in itself.

PART III

UNDERSTANDING YOUR STUDENTS' GOALS AND NEEDS

If your student has been diagnosed with ODD, it is easy to conclude that they are naturally "stubborn" or "difficult," but an honest analysis of a student's behavior should not be swayed by labels. If you try to understand the individual and the specific contexts that happen each day, you will be able to see beyond the stereotypes. Since ODD is a behavioral disorder and not a neurodevelopmental difference, you will have to consider many possible environmental, emotional, and cognitive variables. There is no single "why" when it comes to ODD.

CHAPTER 9

LOOKING FOR THE "WHY" OF BEHAVIOR

One of the most common misconceptions when it comes to students diagnosed with ODD is that these students are deliberately disruptive and hostile, simply preprogrammed to say "no" to anything you request. When students are not aligned with your agenda, it's tempting to take things personally and jump to conclusions. "This student is just being oppositional" is a deceptive but convenient fallback, and does nothing to answer the question "Why is this student pushing back when asked to follow school expectations?" Worse yet, false assumptions can stoke feelings of anger and resentment, and justify harsh disciplinary measures that trigger even more defiance and opposition. To break that destructive cycle, it's essential to understand the individual factors that contribute to your students' struggles at school.

For example, you might see a student whose forehead has been firmly pressed to the desk for the first 20 minutes of class and assume that:

- This student is unmotivated, stubborn, and only cares about video games.
- They are trying to make a point, showing contempt.
- They are trying to make it impossible to be taught, and doesn't want to learn.

What else could it be? Here are a few other possibilities:

- This student was up late last night / couldn't fall asleep / was chatting with friends for support with a personal problem that is affecting their mental health.
- They have difficulty with organization / anxiety about losing things / forgot to bring a notebook today but are embarrassed to tell you.
- This student is distracted / frustrated because time keeps slipping by, despite their best intentions.
- They are lonely / have been trying to connect with classmates but feels intimidated and hopeless.

As you can see, there are so many different struggles that can look quite similar on the surface. Understanding the exact nature of the struggle will certainly help you cultivate an empathetic attitude and build a stronger connection with your student, but there is also a practical advantage to looking deeper beneath the surface—when you understand the struggle, you can help to address it. Instead of trying to increase motivation or instill fear, you will be able to work with your student to identify the stumbling block, and then start moving it aside. Looking back to the student with their head down on their desk, here are some supports you can offer if you understand the nature of the problem that the student is facing:

- If your student is losing sleep due to worry and stress, you can suggest resources such as counseling or talk to them about ways to find help for mental health without sacrificing sleep.
- If they have difficulty with organizing their materials or remembering daily tasks, you can strategize together to organize reminders and back-up plans, and share resources for students struggling with executive functioning deficits.
- If your student is having trouble focusing and feeling frustrated due to ongoing distractions, you will be able to problem-solve with them to help them self-regulate with strategies such as movement breaks or you can help them find ways to screen out intrusive noises or activities.
- If your student is burdened with loneliness, you can arrange activities that include more social interaction, or invite specific students to sit nearby and discuss preferred topics.

FINDING THE "WHY" OF BEHAVIOR

Now that we have started to think about the student's perspective and how their needs and goals might influence classroom behavior, how do you go about narrowing it down and then deciding what to do about it? If your student has been diagnosed with ODD, it is easy to conclude that they are naturally "stubborn" or "difficult," but an honest analysis of a student's behavior should not be swayed by labels. If you try to understand the individual and the specific contexts that happen each day, you will be able to see beyond the stereotype. Since ODD is a behavioral disorder and not a neurodevelopmental difference, you will have to consider many possible environmental, emotional, and cognitive variables. There is no single "why" when it comes to ODD.

The phrase "All behavior is communication" might be a familiar one to you, and many educators have found this to be a useful approach (even if it is not literally true). The question of "why" is extremely important, because without understanding the reason for the behavior, we cannot analyze the triggers or offer a reasonable replacement for the behavior. In other words, without the "why," any intervention we attempt is likely to be superficial and not very effective.

Despite the importance of the "why" of behavior, most people spend more time thinking about the exact form of the behavior, the damage it caused, and how it made them feel. At school, the formal consequence or disciplinary measures taken are usually in direct proportion to how disruptive or damaging the behavior was, and assigned based on the type of disruptive behavior (e.g., aggression, verbal outbursts, property damage, truancy).

Alice Klassen, an educator and formerly a student with oppositional and defiant tendencies, shared a story of what happened when her teachers did not look very far for the "why" of her behavior:

> The teachers seemed to be really concerned about things that didn't matter to me. For example, we all had to wear these navy blue knee socks as part of the school uniform. We would get in trouble if they slipped down, so I was always pulling them up. The elastic in the socks was old and had broken down, so I actually had calluses on my knuckles from pulling up these socks so many times a day. I still got detention from the teachers because of those stupid socks. Fortunately, the teachers sent me to an old auditorium in the quietest part of the school to serve the detention, and I just had to sit there for a while. I remember actually enjoying the peace and silence in that room.
>
> Eventually I felt like I couldn't escape the criticism, so I decided to lean into it. I just felt like my teachers were out to get me. They probably thought I was a disaster, and I guess I was. This was years before my ADHD diagnosis. Anyway, I wasn't really successful at conforming, so I decided to go in the opposite direction. I invented weird pranks to play, like hiding a tape player in my bag and playing an audio recording of a rainstorm during class. Our school uniform had very specific rules about how short our skirts could be, but no one had informed us of the maximum length, so I scoured the shops for a floor-length navy skirt. I got such a kick out of swooshing down the halls in that skirt, knowing there was nothing in the rule book to stop me. I heard they actually did put in a clause about that after I left, which made me feel very proud. I think I also tried to invent an alternate form of 'shoes.'

When a disciplinary consequence does not address the underlying issue, the problem behavior tends to persist and can even worsen. In this example, no one asked why the student's socks were falling down. The consequence did nothing to solve the problem, and the time she spent in detention was not a deterrent. However, the student responded to this arbitrary approach with a sense of hopelessness and, eventually, rebellion.

CHALLENGES AND OPPORTUNITIES IN THE SEARCH FOR ANSWERS

Without a fair and informed process for understanding the "why" of behavior, it is easy to jump to conclusions. Perhaps Alice Klassen's teachers decided that she did not care to please them, or that she was deliberately flouting the school rules. Every teacher will have impressions and judgments, but these must be weighed alongside other types of assessments.

As a teacher, you can borrow techniques from many different professional fields to help you understand your students. The last few decades have brought an explosion of new research and insight about child development, pedagogy, motivation, stress, self-regulation, attachment, and leadership. In every field, old assumptions have been upended. If you were confident about something you learned even five years ago, there has probably been some research since then challenging that notion. On the subject of human behavior, there is still much more to learn, and many questions we have not even thought to ask yet.

In other words, science does not stand still. Fields of research that were once impossible to reconcile are expanding outward, and as they grow, they start to overlap. The most gifted clinicians I have ever met are often the ones who listen closely to colleagues in other fields, borrowing, adapting, exploring, and absorbing knowledge. We are so fortunate to live at this juncture in history. We can learn what has been proven to be true, but we can also learn from the mistakes of the past. From our vantage point, we can see how easy it is to make too many assumptions, to try to explain too much with just a handful of facts.

With this humbling knowledge in mind, I will do my best to familiarize you with how different fields have sought to understand the "why" of behavior, and to point you toward some useful practical tools you can use to understand the individual "why" of your students' behavior.

FINDING PREDICTABLE PATTERNS IN BEHAVIOR: FUNCTIONAL ASSESSMENTS

"Functional assessments" are a commonly used tool for analyzing patterns of behavior and testing hypotheses to understand how a person's behavior is interacting with their environment. The functional assessment works on the assumption that behavior persists for a reason. That is to say, behavior (challenging or otherwise) usually *meets a need of some kind*. To put it in familiar terms once again: "behavior is communication." This position might seem obvious to modern readers, but at the beginning of the 20th century, psychology did not yet have a framework for how learning occurs aside from the most basic conditioning processes. Psychoanalysis (including the study of dreams and the collective unconscious) asked questions about the "why" of behavior, but its methods were more speculative than scientific. Traditional beliefs about spirituality, bodily humors, and family lineage persisted as possible answers to the "why" of behavior, and over the next few generations, the study of psychology would struggle to bridge a widening gap between the study of the "mind" and the "body."

By the middle of the 20th century, "behaviorism" emerged as a promising way to understand and predict behavior with a certain degree of rigor. Researchers synthesized findings from animal testing to build a framework that might systematically explain how the learning environment can alter animal behavior. Specifically, researchers were demonstrating the principles of "operant conditioning." In the simplest possible terms, "operant conditioning" is at work when an organism emits a behavior, receives a rewarding consequence, and proceeds to

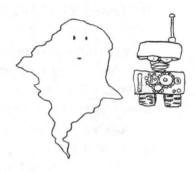

emit that behavior more frequently. Through operant learning, organisms can learn to spot the signs that a reward is on the way, or navigate around an object if it has been previously associated with punishment. B. F. Skinner is justly known as the founder of "behaviorism," and his work stood out as exceptional for two reasons.

First, he was able to use these newly established principles of learning to subtly change animal behavior in very unexpected ways (have a look at his work on teaching pigeons to play ping-pong for a memorable demonstration[1]). Skinner designed and built machines that responded in predictable ways when animals interacted with them. He then recorded his subjects' behavior as they interacted with the machines, and noted how those behaviors changed as the programming of the machines was adjusted. Through experimentation, Skinner (1957) demonstrated that animals responded in predictable ways to these powerful, precisely tuned environments, and he described how planned changes in the environment can shape the behavior of an organism to almost any ends. He also helped build the groundwork for modern self-led learning with his "teaching machine," a mechanical apparatus designed to provide positive reinforcement when students provide correct responses.

Skinner was also notable for a second reason: he recognized the immense practical potential of "operant conditioning" on organisms of all kinds, and he speculated about how it could be used to better humanity by shaping human behavior on a much larger scale.

By the 1970s, schools and homes all over the English-speaking world were applying a selection of behavioral principles, also known as *behavior modification*, to shape the behavior of the children in their care. However, these systems of rewards and punishments were designed to shape behavior, not to understand it. For the purposes of running an efficient classroom or a home, this approach was considered quite sufficient.

Not all behavior is so easily manipulated, however, and in hospitals and mental institutions, where people with developmental disabilities or mental illness were routinely confined, patients who engaged in self-injury and other dangerous or persistently maladaptive behavior were subjected to inhumane and brutal treatment (Ayllon & Michael 1959). It was in this context that the first forms of "functional assessment" emerged, assuming that understanding of the "why" of this behavior could help to address behaviors of concern. After all, "behaviorism" had demonstrated that living things respond to their environments, so perhaps an experimental approach could point to a kind of rationale or reason why the behavior persists.

Instead of simply ascribing difficult behavior to some kind of fault or basic problem with the individual, clinicians began to act on the assumption that the maladaptive behavior might be helping the individual access or avoid something significant. In one of the first published studies on the "function" of behavior, researchers demonstrated that instead of contriving rewards and punishments, clinicians could offer patients an alternative way to fulfill the purpose (or "function") of their behavior while reducing the "payoff" for the maladaptive behavior (Iwata *et al.* 1982). For example, if a patient was screaming and throwing chairs, clinicians could use a functional assessment to try

1   See www.youtube.com/watch?v=vGazyH6fQQ4

to understand the "why" of this behavior. After observing and recording the behavior in different conditions, the data might show that this behavior tended to happen in the presence of a particular staff member (let's call him "Steve"), and usually stopped when that staff member was removed. Working on the hypothesis that *escape from the staff member* was the function of the behavior, clinicians could offer the patient an alternative behavior that serves the same purpose, such as saying "Steve, go." If the patient could say "Steve, go" and achieve the same result with less effort, then the screaming and throwing of chairs would no longer serve the same important purpose.

In 1982, Dr Brian Iwata and his team published the first formal method for testing a functional hypothesis to confirm the "why" of a behavior. They proposed that by following this procedure, teams could systematically test whether a specific behavior served one of four different functions: escape, access to tangibles, attention, and automatic/sensory. This method was based solely on observing the patient's behavior across a range of carefully arranged situations. It had the advantage of being quite objective, since the function of the behavior would be determined by counting how many times it occurred in a given setting. This type of functional assessment, often referred to as a "functional analysis," was designed to be used with both speaking and nonspeaking individuals.

Possible functions of behavior	Description
Access to tangibles	The goal of the behavior might be access to a preferred object or activity. When this problem behavior happens, does the student get access to something preferred? Does the behavior seem to be directed toward getting something?
Automatic/sensory	The goal of the behavior might be a pleasant or interesting feeling, or provide a sense of relief from pain. When this problem behavior happens, is there a sensory component? Does the behavior feel good, or provide relaxation or an interesting sensation?
Escape	As suggested by the name, the goal of the behavior could be to get away from something unpleasant, like a painful sound or an irritating task. When this problem behavior happens, does the student get away from something nonpreferred? Does the behavior seem to help to avoid unpleasant things?
Attention	The goal of the behavior is social—an attempt to connect with or get help from another person. When this problem behavior happens, does the student attract attention from others? Does it seem designed to invite attention from others?

Functional assessments have been successfully used to suggest an effective treatment when a replacement behavior is urgently needed, especially in cases where communication with the patient is limited and the behavior is self-injury or highly aggressive. However, it is harder to use traditional functional assessments in cases where the behavior either is extremely frequent in all kinds of conditions, or in contrast, it happens only very rarely.

In 1989, the passage of the Individuals with Disabilities Education Act (IDEA) mandated that American schools should provide a formal Functional Behavior Assessment (FBA) before changing the school placement of a student with disabilities. In practice, this is not always the case. School policies with "zero tolerance" for violence and threats may conflict with this process, and some schools do not have access to clinicians who can provide a formal FBA.

In an effort to gain a more objective perspective, some teachers and consultants rely on observations, collected and organized into discrete "incidents." These can be described in terms of the lead-up, the behavior, and the aftermath (also known as the antecedent, behavior, and consequence, or ABC). You may have seen this type of data collection or heard of "ABC data."

Generally speaking, there are some clues to be found by inspecting the lead-up to difficult behaviors (such as possible triggers, contributing factors, and pressures) and in the aftermath (results that lead to relief or advantage.) Tracking these patterns and looking at the variables can be an extremely useful practice, but there are some limitations to be aware of. The immediate context of the behavior is important, but teachers are not always able to observe all the events that can shape behavior both before and after.

The "why" of behavior can be hard to spot on an "ABC data sheet" in cases where:

- Important trigger points happen out of view
- Incidents are severe but happen infrequently
- Past events impact current behavior
- Thoughts, feelings, and sensations change the significance of events
- Other important events are happening at the same time.

Methodologies have since been developed to capture more subtle, individual behavior goals and to make it more practical to test them. For example, Dr Gregory Hanley's tool, the IISCA (Interview-Informed Synthesized Contingency Analysis; see Hanley *et al.* 2014), collects information using interviews as well as observation, and tests scenarios that are specific to the client.

In terms of specific tools to use in the classroom, Jessica Minahan and Nancy Rappaport's excellent book *The Behavior Code* (2012) uses the functional assessment as a starting point to help teachers notice behavior patterns, but is also written from a trauma-informed perspective, and includes important information about mental health topics such as anxiety and sexualized behavior.

THE COLLABORATIVE AND PROACTIVE SOLUTIONS (CPS) APPROACH

The simplest assessment and the most natural place to start in the search for the "why" of a behavior is with the student. We can listen to what they have been telling us, and ask them questions. If they are nonspeaking and do not use a means of augmentative and alternative communication (AAC), we can look at their emotional responses and pay attention to what they avoid and what they choose. While essential, these conversations are often difficult and incomplete. If we are lucky, students will share their feelings and ideas with us, but still they may not understand the bigger patterns or fully explain their own responses. The Collaborative and Proactive Solutions (CPS) approach, developed by Dr Ross Greene, works by engaging patients in conversation to define and address the "unsolved problems" that lead to challenging behavior (see Booker *et al.* 2019). As a psychologist working in juvenile detention facilities and psychiatric inpatient units, Dr Greene saw that seclusion and restraints were being used alongside token reward systems to manage dangerous patient behavior, without much success. Dr Greene subsequently developed a version of the CPS to use in classrooms or as a school-wide system for responding to challenging behavior: "In the CPS model, challenging behaviors are viewed merely as the means by which a resident is communicating that he or she is having difficulty meeting certain expectations" (Greene 2018).

Like most functional assessments, CPS aims to uncover reasons behind challenging behavior. When the adult and the child have expressed their view of the issue, they generate and negotiate solutions together. Like the IISCA, the CPS process works by gathering information through conversations with the student, analyzing the situations where problems tend to occur, and assessing the student's skills in areas like problem-solving. However, rather than viewing the behavior in terms of its inter-action with the environment (like antecedents and consequences), CPS focuses more on understanding a child's behavior in the context of their developmental process, as summarized in a document called the *Assessment of Lagging Skills and Unsolved Problems* (ALSUP), which can be accessed in Dr Greene's book *Lost at School* (2008).

THE BIOPSYCHOSOCIAL MODEL

The biopsychosocial model is an interdisciplinary framework that emphasizes the interconnected nature of biological, psychological, and social systems. In terms of understanding classroom behavior, the biopsychosocial model should always be reviewed to ensure that physical health, mental health, and community connections are supported (Dodge & Pettit 2003). Students must be able to meet their basic needs as a prerequisite before conforming to school expectations. For example, an intervention to address a student's irritability and lack of focus in the classroom will be more successful if the student is also able to get a good night's sleep without worrying about their parent's drug addiction. A plan to curb the number of times a student leaves the classroom will be more successful if the teachers are aware of any medical issues, such as bladder infections or Crohn's disease.

Important needs	Examples	
Biological: physical traits, needs, illness, disability	• Access to food, water, and shelter • Air and water quality at home • Sleep habits • Basic safety • Genetic conditions • Genetic susceptibility • Brain injury • Developmental delays • Dental pain or illness	• Addiction • Chronic pain • Eating disorders • Vitamin deficiencies • Tics and other atypical movement patterns • Drug use • Pharmaceutical treatment • Hormonal imbalances

Psychological: cognitive and emotional characteristics	• Social skills • Coping skills • Stress vulnerability • Anxiety • Depression • Executive functioning skills	• Learning disabilities • Attachment disorders • Personal beliefs • Values • Preferences
Social and community: resources and connections in the family and neighborhood	• Cultural values • Parental support • Parental discipline • Parent employment • Family lifestyle • Extended family support • Siblings	• Socioeconomic status • Acceptance of differences • Crime rate • Peer influence • Social rejection • Academic success

STRESS, EMOTION, AND NEUROBIOLOGICAL CONNECTIONS

While behavioral researchers analyzed changes in the physical environment to bring about changes in an individual's behavior, some clinicians were approaching behavior in a different way: from the inside out. For example, Dr Mary Ainsworth and Dr John Bowlby set down the foundations of Attachment Theory, tracing the importance of secure emotional connections between children and caregivers, and demonstrating how these relationships resonate powerfully for the individual throughout a lifetime. Meanwhile, other psychologists investigated the "inner" life of emotions, thoughts, memories, and relationships, using both qualitative and quantitative tools to measure their results. By the end of the 20th century, scientists had just begun to articulate the process of "emotional self-regulation" as a complex interplay of physiological responses, chemicals, behaviors, thoughts, and social responses.

Advances in medical technology opened up new avenues of inquiry into the body itself, and researchers began to watch changes in brain activity and skin reactivity in real time. Neurobiological research suggested deeper questions about the "why" of behavior. Neurobiological research may help to tie together factors that influence the "why" of behavior, from genetics and brain development to relationships and trauma. In 1994, Dr Stephen Porges brought a neurobiological perspective to the theory of attachment and proposed polyvagal theory to explain how our neurological systems develop through nurturing relationships with caregivers (Porges 2005). Polyvagal theory has emerged as a plausible explanation for the important links between our nervous systems, our social relationships, and our ability to emotionally self-regulate. These links might help to partly explain the biological reasons behind why some children seem to be hard to soothe, hard to connect with, or "differently wired," as Debra Reber would say (2019).

Polyvagal theory suggests that when children cannot reliably access comfort and co-regulation from safe adults, either because they are physiologically dysregulated or because the relationships are disrupted, the child is obliged to spend more time in a state of dysregulation and stress. Consequently, the child spends less time in social learning, inquiry, and relationship-building. Dr Daniel J. Siegel and Dr Tina Payne Bryson have authored many popular books aimed at parents, to help them understand how to support emotional self-regulation in lieu of more traditional disciplinary or "behavior management" approaches (see, for example, Siegel & Bryson 2012).

This form of support is especially important for sensitive students as they develop their logical reasoning or social skills. When these students experience stress, their intellectual or relational problems become even harder to solve, and the cycle can soon start spinning out of control. Consider this dilemma the next time you are faced with a child who "will not see reason" and who does not respond to the typical attempts to calm and console.

The most basic emotional process is the ability to discern a threat from an opportunity. This process, known as *neuroception*, is like a filter that sorts out everything we encounter (Porges 2009). It happens continuously, as we meet people and decide whether they are friendly, or when we hear a sound and decide whether it is dangerous. When a child is responding to you in an aggressive way, shouting and throwing things, remember that even your logic and support might be mistaken for a threat by a child with unreliable neuroception.

To a student in an escalated emotional state, everything can feel like a potential threat. When difficult tasks, sensations, demands, and interactions are filtered and labeled as a "threat," the student will treat these challenges as problems to be avoided or attacked, not as complex puzzles to be resolved. In this way, emotional reactivity can be a contributing factor to other concerns, such as academic challenges, sensory processing issues, attentional issues, and social relationships.

These challenges can overlap throughout the day, so be on the lookout for:

- Unfamiliar situations
- Uncertainty and unstructured time
- Difficult academic tasks
- Transitions between activities
- Sensory overwhelm or under-stimulation
- Physical needs such as lack of sleep
- Social rejection
- Noise levels
- Visual clutter.

For students who are already quite sensitive to stress, a "controlling" classroom can be a challenging environment. One study examined the stress responses of people performing a puzzle task (Reeve & Tseng 2011), and compared their cortisol levels (a hormone associated with stress) when they were given controlling feedback versus neutral or autonomy-supporting feedback. Unsurprisingly, people who experienced the controlling feedback tested higher for signs of stress. Obviously, reducing student stress would be beneficial for student wellness, but there is also an obvious link between stress reactions and disruptive behavior. If you can incorporate more autonomy-supporting practices into your whole classroom, you are not only supporting student engagement; you are also likely to see fewer outbursts and acts of "defiance" from students.

Unfortunately, most clinicians are still categorized as working with either bodies *or* minds, and many explanations for behavior largely ignore one side or the other. This is probably due more to the way university departments are structured than to any real irreconcilable gap between the fields of knowledge. These days, doctors, psychologists, behavior analysts, social workers, occupational therapists, and educators have access to the same research literature, use many of the same tools, and have a growing language in common, although there is still a long way to go before we have integrated the knowledge from across these fields.

Let's start with an example from a middle school classroom, and see what questions will lead us to understanding this student's needs and goals, which could then point to an effective solution to the school problem.

D'Artagnan is a middle school student. His teacher, Ms Aimes, has heard from other teachers that he is a kid who is always eager to chat but not very academically serious.

His student record shows that he has had some contact with the police, but so far he has only been warned in connection to making threats toward another student. Psycho-educational testing shows that he has some strengths in verbal reasoning, but has difficulty with working memory and processing speed.

His teacher notices that he often arrives fairly late to math class after lunch, and then asks permission to leave "to get something from his locker." After leaving the room, D'Artagnan is gone for about 10 minutes. Other teachers report that he sometimes walks laps around the school. When he returns, he has usually missed the instructions for the assignment. This seems to be happening more and more often.

D'Artagnan's teacher has tried giving him reminders to bring his materials to class promptly, and she has even denied permission (he just argues, then leaves the class anyway). Ms Aimes has no choice but to wait for him to return, and usually ends up sitting with him to explain the math assignment so he can catch up with the class. She is thinking of sending an email to the family if the situation does not improve.

Let's go back to Ms Aimes' classroom and look at D'Artagnan's behavior using some perspectives commonly used in schools.

Using a traditional functional assessment to understand the "why" of D'Artagnan's behavior

To better understand what purpose D'Artagnan's walks during math class might serve, Ms Aimes could start by recording some observations to help narrow down the possibilities. Does this behavior happen every single day, or only on certain days? What is different on days when he comes to class on time? A daily log would be very helpful in narrowing this down. In looking at the daily logs, and in conversation with D'Artagnan, Ms Ames might look for the answers to questions such as:

- Does this behavior result in something fun and interesting? [Automatic/sensory]
- Does this behavior attract attention from others? [Attention]

- Does this behavior help to avoid something unpleasant? [Escape]
- Does this behavior result in gaining something? [Access to tangibles]

Using the CPS to find the "why" of D'Artagnan's behavior

To better understand which expectations D'Artagnan is struggling to meet, and what unsolved problems he might be struggling with, Ms Aimes could approach D'Artagnan and follow the steps outlined by Dr Greene in his books (including *The Explosive Child*). The four steps of the process, roughly summarized, are:

- The teacher approaches the student with empathy and without blame, listening to their concerns and point of view.
- The teacher then explains why this issue is of concern (e.g., safety, harm to student or others).
- The teacher invites the student to propose some possible solutions that would result in a "win-win" for both parties.
- The teacher and student arrive at an agreement, and make a plan to try out the solution, and then meet again to discuss the results.

Using a biopsychosocial approach to find the "why" of D'Artagnan's behavior

To better understand which needs D'Artagnan might be struggling to meet, taking into account the broader context of his life, Ms Aimes could ask herself:

- What could this student be moving *toward*?
- What could this student be moving *away from*?

	Question	Possible answers
Biological	What do I know about D'Artagnan's physical needs and health?	Needs extra movement? Does he eat lunch?
Psychological	What do I know about D'Artagnan's thinking style, desires, preferences, and goals?	Possible learning disability? Enjoys socializing? Needs extra support during class?
Social	What do I know about D'Artagnan's home and community?	What happens at lunchtime? Who does he spend time with? Are there conflicts with peers over lunch hour?

Instead of assuming that D'Artagnan is simply disorganized or uninterested in math, Ms Aimes tries to look at the problem in more depth, imagining possible needs and preferences in as much detail as possible. From what she knows of D'Artagnan's situation, what *needs or desires* might be met via this behavior? What could he be trying to *avoid*?

She starts to speculate again and makes two lists:

What could this student be moving *toward*?	What could this student be moving *away from*?
Friends in the hallway	A student in class
Friends in another class	Crowded spaces
A chance to move	Listening to math instructions
A chance to be alone	Time in math class
Fresh air	Sitting still
Quiet	Strong smell coming from students after gym
More one-on-one time with the teacher	An uncomfortable desk
Lunch alone	Tension with classmates

Instead of jumping to conclusions and forming beliefs about D'Artagnan's willingness to cooperate and succeed in math class, Ms Aimes does her best to look deeper. She does not wait for a formal behavior assessment, but she does jot down what she notices when D'Artagnan comes into the classroom, such as how long it takes, and whether it happens every day.

Before designing a system of incentives or threatening to deliver punishments, Ms Aimes takes D'Artagnan to one side and invites him to talk about his lunch hour. She listens without interrupting, and then asks some follow-up questions for clarity. She asks D'Artagnan: "I'm curious and I'd like to hear your opinion. I keep bugging you about going to your locker because I don't want you to miss the instructions, and I'd like to figure this out. What do you think is getting in the way of you coming to class on time and prepared?"

At first, D'Artagnan says "I dunno," but Ms Aimes waits thoughtfully. D'Artagnan continues: "I guess I just hate coming into the class right after lunch, because it smells in here. Someone always brings fish."

Ms Aimes is surprised, but delighted. This was not on her list of possible ideas, but it is something to work with. "Wow! Thank you for telling me that! I wonder if there's a way for us to solve that problem." D'Artagnan grins and says he will think about it, but the bell for the next class rings and the conversation is over for now.

The search for the "why" of behavior is rarely a simple one, and there are no tools that are perfect in any situation. Ms Aimes didn't remember perfectly what she had learned at various training workshops, but her goal was to understand D'Artagnan a little better. She succeeded in keeping an open mind, and collecting some useful information from her own observations and from D'Artagnan himself. She now has something to work on with D'Artagnan, and even if it is not the whole solution (he may also have trouble with time management and need extra exercise in order to focus, for example), she has begun the process.

SUMMARY

If your student is breaking the rules and causing disruption in the classroom, you should try to understand why. Behavior happens for a reason. Your student's behavior is affected by many things, including health, other people, and their personal history. If you want their behavior to change, you might need to show them a better way to get what they need, or change something in their environment.

Researchers have tried to find the best way to understand the "why" of a behavior. When you have a plan to dig deep and uncover why a behavior is happening in a specific situation, this is called a "functional assessment."

You might be able to understand the "why" of a behavior by watching the person carefully to look for patterns. If you notice what usually happens right before the behavior, you might find the trigger or the cue. When you know the trigger or the cue, you can change something about the situation, or practice a different way to react. You can also look at what happens after the behavior. If the behavior helps the student to meet a need or avoid something unpleasant, you can help that student meet the need in a different way. Jessica Minahan and Nancy Rappaport's book *The Behavior Code* can guide you through each step of process, and the worksheets in this book can get you started (see Part IV).

Another way to understand the "why" of behavior is to connect with your student and listen closely to what they have to say. Even if they do not speak, you can use pictures or offer choices to understand what they prefer and what they would like to avoid. When you approach your student with empathy, you can understand the situation from their perspective, and learn more about their strengths and needs. You can also ask them for ideas and suggestions, as you solve the problem together. Dr Ross Greene gives many helpful examples about how to collaborate with your students to understand the "why" of their behavior in his book *Lost at School*.

These two strategies will help you understand your student's specific struggles, but sometimes it helps to look at the big picture too. The biopsychosocial approach will help you look at their life history, community, and health. If your student has had difficult family relationships, traumatic events, or medical problems, they may have different needs than other students. They might need extra help outside of the classroom before they can handle certain challenges at school.

Speaking of challenges, you might find it helpful to look at how your student handles stress. The neurobiological perspective can guide you when they are having big emotional ups and downs. If your student's behavior is connected to feelings of anxiety, overwhelm, or fear, you might want to help them feel safer in your classroom. Dr Mona Delahooke advises parents and teachers on how to connect with stressed-out students in her book *Beyond Behaviours*.

CHAPTER 10

COMMON CLASSROOM STRUGGLES

INVISIBLE DISABILITIES

Won't follow or *can't follow* instructions?

As you have learned, a label of ODD is not strictly an emotional or intellectual disability. Instead, "oppositional" and "defiant" behaviors are usually noticed when an adult places demands on a child. When you encounter a student who is consistently refusing to participate in academic activities, it's easy to jump to conclusions and assume that this is a personal affront, a bid for attention, or showboating in front of peers. The student may not be able to explain why the task is so loathsome, so you are told simply that it is "boring" or "dumb."

If these demands and disruptive responses are happening in an academic setting, you might keep a look-out for some possible academic disabilities or differences that impact the child's ability to learn or stay calm in the classroom. When a child's disability or difference causes academic struggles, the most obvious signs will be refusal, distraction, or defiance.

Your student may not come into your classroom with any other diagnoses, or even the ability to tell you what the struggle is. However, when a child does not follow instructions, it is vital to look closely and ask: *Is this a question of "can't" or "won't"?*

When students present as "typical" (that is, no obvious physical differences or behavioral quirks), they get streamed into typical classrooms, but they may have very uneven skill sets. When students are very advanced in one area (such as verbal ability) and very delayed in another idea (such as working memory), their gifts may be more evident than their struggles. This phenomenon is called "cloaking" because a student appears to be competent overall but quietly strains to keep up. Without a thorough psycho-educational assessment, some learning differences and cognitive barriers can go completely unnoticed. Many teachers arrive in the classroom without training about how to look for invisible learning disabilities, and parents may not have the opportunity to observe their child grappling with this particular problem. This book cannot take the place of regular professional development opportunities, but it may alert you to some areas you can explore more deeply.

In this section, you will find descriptions of some types of invisible disability that, if untreated and unrecognized, can be mistaken for behavioral problems in your classroom.

COLOR VISION DEFICIENCY AND LOW VISION

The most common type of color vision deficiency is known as "red-green color blindness," although there are many variations of this inherited condition. Around one in 12 males have some kind of difference in color perception and one in 200 females.

Classroom difficulties for students with color vision deficiency

Colors are often used in games and to designate classroom organization systems. A student with color vision deficiency may unwittingly take materials from the "wrong" bin, or move a game piece from someone else's team. Out in the play yard, a student with color vision deficiency may struggle to see who is on their team, or spot orange balls against a background of green grass. It may appear that this student is ignoring instructions or cheating, especially if the student has difficulties with attention and inhibition, but be cautious before giving a rebuke in these cases.

Accommodations and accessibility

- Remember that different kinds of light can affect color recognition.
- Give instructions based on shape and pattern, not color.
- Set up preferential seating (good natural light is often ideal).
- Use patterns or shapes to differentiate, rather than color.
- Photocopy worksheets in black and white to see if the task can still be performed.
- When giving paints or art materials, clearly label the colors.
- Use a large, high contrast, sans-serif font when giving presentations on a screen.

DYSCALCULIA

Dyscalculia is a term that describes a specific learning disability in the area of mathematics and arithmetic that cannot be explained by any other difficulty with intelligence, motivation, and opportunity. In other words, some students struggle with a basic "number sense," and this difficulty appears to be related to some specific neurological processes. For example, a student diagnosed with dyscalculia might be quite able to judge two literal quantities to see which one is larger, but would make more errors on a symbolic task, such as comparing two numbers to decide which is bigger.

A student is considered to meet the criteria for dyscalculia if they demonstrate impaired performance on tasks that involve counting and quantities despite typical intelligence, working memory, and vocabulary. There are not yet many studies examining the long-term outcomes and associated characteristics of students diagnosed with dyscalculia, but it appears to be a fairly persistent condition, detectable throughout the lifetime (Shalev & Gross-Tsur 2001). Dyscalculia is thought to affect about 3–6 percent of the population, although the rate is slightly higher among children with other developmental difficulties such as reading problems or ADHD.

If you have a student who appears to be at least two grade levels below expectations in mathematics studies, and you are seeing long solution times, high error rates, and limited problem-solving strategies, then further investigation into dyscalculia is warranted.

Classroom difficulties for students with dyscalculia

Since dyscalculia is a specific learning disability, a student with dyscalculia may perform very well on tasks that involve memory, vocabulary, and logical reasoning, but struggle where numbers are involved. If your student is particularly reluctant to approach mathematical challenges, complains of being "bad at math," or even turns to distraction and disruption during math class, they may have trouble meeting academic expectations. As with any learning disability, it can be hard for students to admit that they do not understand, and they may compare themselves unfavorably with their peers. Some students camouflage their struggles by refusing to try, being silly, or being deliberately defiant, especially when called upon to answer questions in class.

Accommodations and accessibility

- Multi-sensory strategies and concrete learning materials can help compensate for impaired number sense.
- Assess reading to ensure that students can decode written instructions.
- Many parents will willingly provide math tutors for their children, but often mental health struggles such as anxiety are just as debilitating, so access to a counselor or social worker could be a benefit to a student struggling with dyscalculia.

DYSLEXIA

Dyslexia is a common learning disability, estimated to affect 3–7 percent of the population. The diagnosis is given to people who have the opportunity and the desire to learn to read, but struggle despite strengths in other academic areas. Dyslexia is not thought to be a vision problem, but a condition that affects the language processing areas of the brain in specific and measurable ways. Dyslexia can affect spelling, word recognition, and phonological abilities such as generating rhyming words or counting the number of syllables in a word.

Classroom difficulties for students with dyslexia

Children with dyslexia may face stigma and ridicule in the classroom. Difficulty with reading can trigger anxiety and shame, and mask other strengths.

Accommodations and accessibility

- Give verbal instructions.
- Willingly repeat instructions.
- Look for resources with larger print.
- Present material with fewer items per page.
- Use highlighted text.
- Give extra time for reading and providing answers.
- Deliver information in songs or poems.
- Offer text in audio format.

Outside of class, dyslexic children may benefit from intensive, structured interventions such as Multisensory Structured Language Education (MSLE) or Orton–Gillingham (OG).

SENSORY PROCESSING DISORDER

At least one in twenty people may be affected by a sensory processing disorder (SPD). Children with SPD experience the world differently; there is no single profile but many variations of increased or decreased sensitivity. SPDs are more common among children who are also neurodiverse (e.g., diagnosed as gifted, ADHD, Autistic, fragile X syndrome). SPDs are often undiagnosed, and mistaken for behavioral or emotional disorders.

Classroom difficulties for students with SPD

A child with SPD may have very acute senses, so strong smells trigger headaches, loud noises are physically painful, tiny noises are distracting, and/or clothing can feel too tight or too itchy. These children could be called "sensory-avoiding," sometimes withdrawing until the symptoms of over-stimulation trigger an outburst or "meltdown." Busy environments, loud announcements on the speaker, sudden bells, fidgety classmates, glaring lights, or the squeak of the chalk can add up to a very stressful classroom for sensory-avoiding students.

Other children with SPD seem to crave intense sensory experiences, and so tight squeezes and loud noises provide a feeling of relief and relaxation. These "sensory-seeking" children may jostle against other students, chew on objects like pencils or clothing, jump up and down, or lie flat out on the floor. These urges will often conflict with classroom rules with respect to personal space, or the expectation that children will sit quietly at their desks to complete tasks.

Whether under-stimulated or over-stimulated, children with SPD experience a high level of physical stress, and often have difficulty regulating their behavior and emotions in unsuitable environments.

Accommodations and accessibility

- Normalize the use of sensory tools such as fidgets and movement breaks.
- Offer ear defenders.
- Avoid highly scented learning materials.
- Look for ways to add tactile experiences (e.g., sand, water, clay).
- Minimize visual clutter on the walls.
- Try out different lighting schemes (e.g., natural light only, reading lamps, eliminating fluorescent lights if possible, LED lights, tinting lights).
- Provide options for children who need to work in different body positions (e.g., curled up or lying on their stomachs, standing desks).
- Listen closely for squeaks and scrapes, and look for ways to muffle the sound (e.g., padding, oil).
- Pop-up tents can help provide a sense of safety and privacy when overwhelmed.

SUMMARY

Some students diagnosed with oppositional defiant disorder (ODD) need extra help in the classroom because they have learning or sensory differences. If your student is refusing to complete work in class, you might find it hard to see exactly where the problem is. If they are very young, they may not have been diagnosed yet. If they are avoiding certain activities, you can watch out for these differences, and others:

- Color vision deficiency and low vision
- Dyscalculia
- Dysgraphia
- Sensory processing disorder (SPD).

If you understand how these challenges might affect your students, you can set up your classroom to be more accessible. This will help all your learners, even the ones without challenging behavior.

CHAPTER 11

SKILLS THAT IMPROVE COOPERATION IN THE CLASSROOM

So far, this book has focused on helping you discover the needs of individual students so that you can see past the angry mask that is ODD.

You have learned how to look for reasons why your student is struggling, and how to gently connect and build relationships with difficult-to-read students. However, you may be reading this book as a newly certified teacher, or you are reading through it before the start of term in the hope of getting off on the right foot with a new group of students. This section includes teaching practices that you can use with the whole class, even before you face a single power struggle. These are strategies that quietly add up to a more respectful and supportive classroom.

GIVING INSTRUCTIONS THAT ARE BOTH EFFECTIVE AND RESPECTFUL

When speaking to a child, parents and teachers are often warned not to phrase an instruction as a question, such as "Do you want to finish your math sheet?" Presumably, a question like this could invite the child to give an honest answer, and if the answer is "No thanks! I'd rather not," then the adult's intentions have been thwarted. Instead, the adult is encouraged to use a more directive kind of language, such as "You need to finish your math sheet before recess."

Here are some other examples of this type of instruction:

I want everyone to go and line up.
Take your coat off before you sit down.
Stand still during announcements.

These instructions usually take the "imperative" form, which makes it clear to the listener that the adult is not merely making a suggestion. Instructions like this are sometimes referred to as "commands," and the goal of giving an "effective command" is to maximize student compliance (Matheson & Shriver 2005).

There is, of course, a place for giving this kind of instruction as part of a teaching strategy. When a learner is given a simple, specific, positive instruction, they can act on it with more confidence and less confusion. Effective instructions are key when teaching skills that require precision and consistency. For example, competitive athletes, dancers, scuba divers, and surgeons must perform very specific sequences with as few errors as possible, and research has shown that the most effective way to teach these behaviors is with concise, positive, and direct language and immediate positive feedback (Quinn, Miltenberger, & Fogel 2015).

The ability to give effective verbal instructions is both an art and a science. It is all too easy to give instructions that are too long or not specific enough. If you notice that you are struggling to give instructions that your students can follow without repetition or nagging, there are some effective training courses you can take online to refine your technique. One approach that has been demonstrated to be very effective in the research literature with many different populations (not just for children with developmental disabilities) is the TAGteach method.[1]

However, there are limitations to the use of commands in the classroom. When a student responds to a command, there are only two possibilities: a correct response or an incorrect response. Commands do not leave room for debate, feedback, negotiation, or creativity. Commands do not invite the student to think or problem-solve.

Commands are ideal for situations where there is only one acceptable response, but this implies that the teacher is responsible for deciding which responses are acceptable and which are unacceptable. This perspective is reinforced in other kinds of direct instructions, such as:

I want you to _____. (Implication: You must do what I want.)
You need to _____. (Implication: I decide what you need.)

This strategy can backfire when addressing students who resist control and value independence (Coyne & Cairns 2016).

One teacher gave an example of her student's unexpected reaction when she gave a "command" to a student diagnosed with ODD:

One of the most challenging (and fascinating) experiences I had as a teacher was the year I spent with a small group of boys in their early teens. They each came with a handful of medical diagnoses, including Tourette's syndrome, chronic fatigue syndrome, autism spectrum disorder, attention deficit disorder, and of course oppositional defiant disorder.

My usual mode of speech is not very directive, so I usually spoke to the students in a very gentle way. For example, I found myself using phrases like "I would suggest that you finish this part first," or "In my opinion, it would make sense to..." instead of blunt directives.

The students responded well to this approach, and we worked out our differences

---

[1] You can find a free introductory course at: www.tagteach.com/Free-TAGteach-course

in a friendly way. I hadn't realized what an impact my language would have until one day, I slipped up.

That morning, time was running short, and I switched to a very direct tone for just a moment. I rapped my fingers on the desk of one particular student, lowered my voice and ordered him to "Get it done!" I meant this as a joke, but I saw him turn to me with a look that immediately told me I had made a mistake. His fingers curled into fists; he straightened and stared at me. This student had a reputation for getting very angry and out of control with other teachers, but he had never lost his temper in my class so far.

I realized that my tone had completely missed the mark, so I cleared my throat and tried again: "What I mean is: if we get this done before 11 o'clock, we'll have time to play our board game." He melted back into his previous relaxed attitude. The switch was so fast, I couldn't believe it.

This teacher had stumbled on the value of "declarative language." Declarative language, as described by Linda K. Murphy in her excellent book *The Declarative Language Handbook: Using a Thoughtful Language Style to Help Kids with Social Learning Challenges Feel Competent, Connected and Understood* (2020), is a way of giving valuable information to students without directly "telling them what to do."[2]

Declarative language is a gentle way to guide a student's attention, and let them choose what to do next (Piazza *et al.* 1997). Reeve calls it "informational, non-pressuring language" (2016, p.131). Declarative language usually takes the form of a comment or a remark. It provides some perspective or some information, but it doesn't imply a demand. It leaves room for differing opinions.

When you use declarative language, you are speaking for yourself and representing your own position.

Your preferences and opinions	Your experiences and observations	Your thoughts and ideas
"I was hoping…" "I would really like to…" "I'm ready for…" "My favorite way to do this is…"	"You look full of energy today!" "I think I just heard a pencil drop on the floor." "I notice that no one is using the side table right now." "I checked the weather this morning, and it's freezing!" "It's really peaceful in this room today."	"I wonder…" "I bet…" "I see…" "I noticed…" "I'm curious about…" "I'm trying to decide…"

TROUBLE-SHOOTING

Using declarative language in your classroom can help to cut down on the number of daily commands you issue. Declarative language has also been shown to cut down on student push-back and refusal. Most importantly, declarative language can be an

---

2   For samples and resources on declarative language, see: www.declarativelanguage.com/free-downloads

excellent opportunity for students to practice making inferences, looking for information, and considering other perspectives.

Students who struggle with executive functioning skills or social skills are especially in need of these learning opportunities, but they might have the most trouble responding to indirect prompts at first. Many of them diagnosed with ODD would also meet the criteria for a diagnosis of ADHD, so they have poor working memory, difficulty switching focus, and impulsive tendencies These students often struggle in situations with loose structure and unclear expectations, because they don't remember the details of the instructions or they simply don't know where to begin.

Fortunately, you can still make declarative language work for your students.

Help for students who can't remember what to do next

Rather than using your voice to give instructions one at a time, use pictures or written instructions so that your students can refer to the instructions at their own pace. For example, when your student looks to you for the information (e.g., "Miss, where are the markers?") this is an opportunity to use declarative thinking instead of a direct prompt. According to Dr Russell Barkley, students who have ADHD sometimes don't hear their "inner voice" as clearly as their typical peers, so they struggle to "talk themselves through" a problem (2006, p.134).

Your declarative language can be a way for your students to develop their own helpful "inner voice." If you were to point and say, "The instructions are over there! I wrote them all out for you. You just have to listen!" the student might conclude that (a) you are the source of information, and (b) you are exasperated by their ignorance.

Instead, try to put yourself in the shoes of your student and reflect out loud:

Hmm, there was something about markers on the instructions I wrote. Where did I put those instructions?

This prompts the student to look around for that information without being directly told. Instead of spoon-feeding the instructions, you have empowered them to find their own answers.

Help for students who struggle with open-ended tasks

Here is an example. Jamie is staring at a blank page, and waves his arm at the teacher. "Sir, I don't know what I should write."

Mr Gupta tries to be more specific: "I asked you to write about what you did last weekend."

Jamie complains: "I didn't do anything! I can't remember. I have nothing to write."

Mr Gupta tries to be encouraging and allow for creativity: "Just use your imagination!"

Jamie lets out a heavy sigh and taps his pencil on the table, but does not reply.

Unfortunately, Mr Gupta's good intentions are undermined by his instructions, which have been delivered in the form of commands. If Jamie is worried about doing things "right" or can't decide which idea to pursue, this advice is not very helpful. Jamie's anxiety levels continue to rise. What else can Mr Gupta say that will allow Jamie to complete the writing task without telling him exactly what to do?

Here are some declarative statements that might help Mr Gupta guide Jamie through the process of thinking what he did that weekend:

> Hmm. When I can't remember something, it helps me to close my eyes and start at the beginning, like I'm watching a movie.
> I wonder if there are any pictures on your phone that would remind you?
> That does sound hard. It would be funny, though, if you just wrote about the most boring weekend ever. That might work!

These declarative statements don't force Jamie to choose a right or wrong answer, and he is free to reject any of the ideas Mr Gupta suggests and suggest his own.

Help for hesitant students

If a student is waiting to be prompted, nudged, and reminded every step of the way, then declarative language might not hit the mark at first. When they find it hard to relate to peers or they have had painful experiences with making mistakes in the past, they often lose confidence and wait for explicit instructions from someone in authority.

If you notice that your student is stalled and looking to you for assurance, you might be very tempted to break the tension and just give the instructions. If your student is genuinely stuck, then it may not hurt to offer some direction, but you are working on building self-efficacy and initiative with this student, so here is some declarative language you can use:

> I see that you are getting ready to start!
> You look a little worried.
> It can be hard to keep moving if you're not sure of the answer.
> I've seen you tackle things like this before.
> This reminds me of the time you solved a similar problem.

SUMMARY

Declarative language is a gentle way to speak to your students and give them the information they need. Students diagnosed with oppositional defiant disorder (ODD) might prefer to hear what they need to know in this style. Instead of giving orders, you simply state facts. For example, you can describe what you see: "I see that most of you are ready to go!" When you use declarative language, you can pause and let the students think about what you have said. When students hear declarative language, they do not have to choose whether to obey or disobey. This is a helpful strategy for students who hate to be told what to do. Declarative language will also help you to avoid power struggles with your students, because you do not have to worry about what to do when they ignore your command.

THE 10 ~~COMMANDMENTS~~ SUGGESTIONS FOR TEACHING STUDENTS DIAGNOSED WITH ODD

There are plenty of big ideas and theories mentioned in this book, but this section is a little different. Within the following list, you will find 10 pieces of advice that have been distilled many different sources and experiences, so you can consume them in concentrated form.

1. **Do not** *offer dire choices or false premises:* "Would you like your friends to fail the test?" As Jessica Minahan and Nancy Rappaport explain in their book *The Behavior Code*, it's important to offer choices, but be sure not to ask your student to choose between the sensible and the ridiculous. For example, do not ask a child to choose between quickly putting on their winter jacket or going outside with no jacket at all. To you it may seem like putting on the jacket is the only possible response, but your students may surprise you. A child with a long history of conflict with adults will often choose the unexpected option, perhaps out of curiosity, or possibly in the hope that you will not follow through.

2. **Do not** *assume that your student will act in self-preservation:* In a moment of escalated stress, the usual reasoning skills and avoidance instincts do not apply. You can warn and you can explain, but if you allow a child to make a self-destructive choice in the hopes of learning from natural consequences, you will likely be disappointed by the results. Instead, a student who is surprised and distressed by the outcome might blame you instead of learning an important lesson.

3. **Do not** *resort to intimidation:* A child who is threatened may rise to the occasion, and assert independence by physically pushing you, feigning violence to scare you off, or making vile threats. Do not put yourself into a situation where your only choices are physically imposing yourself or backing off. Be on the lookout for signs of post-traumatic stress or extreme fight, flight, or freeze responses, and make it your priority to provide both physical and emotional safety. Many of us were taught to expect or display a submissive response such as an apology or looking at the floor, but it might, in fact, just be a socially appropriate way to escape from your dominant display, not recognition that a moral wrong has been corrected (Walker 2009).

4. **Do** *find a quality to like and admire in every student:* Even when you are completely frazzled with a student, remember to keep the positive in mind. The traits and behaviors that you find hardest to deal with are often actually strengths in

disguise. The next time you find yourself the target of some truly repellent name-calling, you can pause to admire the creativity or courage this might have taken. You can appreciate the strength of their convictions, their persistence, their sensitivity, and their willingness to stand up for themselves, among many other things.

5. **Do take responsibility for your own emotional reactions:** No one can blame you for wanting the chance to deliver a really successful lesson when you've worked so hard on putting it together. It's natural to want to see a positive response from students when you are trying your best to be fair and approachable. When you encounter a student whose objections throw a wrench in the works, or who seems to get prickly for no apparent reason, this can hit a sore spot and trigger a painful emotional response for you. Your biggest emotional responses are probably connected to your values. For example, if you value respect, then rudeness can rile you. If you value acceptance, then rejection stings. Be aware of your sensitive spots, so you can assess the situation while taking your own reaction into account.

6. **Do connect before giving an instruction:** Some students seem to be able to just "snap to it" and immediately obey, but if they have a diagnosis of ODD, chances are good that this is not the case. When you need to give an instruction to a student, and you are not sure what the response will be (perhaps the student has a history of ignoring or refusing), you can choose to break the ice a little first. You can even check to see what their objections might be beforehand, by previewing the task, for example, "I'm not asking yet, but I'm thinking of asking you to... How does that sound to you?" If your student wants to protest, you can listen and address those concerns without the emotional urgency that might come with a child who has just heard a command they do not want to obey.

7. **Do make it easy for students to get what they want (without having to break the rules):** If they seem to be getting up and walking around too often, daydreaming at length, or taking far too long in the toilets, and your reminders and rules are not effective, you might be in for an uphill battle. Sometimes students who cannot get their needs met with mild rule-breaking end up resorting to more disruptive methods of protest. For example, the student who gets over-stimulated in class but cannot take breaks may decide to stop coming to school altogether, or take an unscheduled field trip when your back is turned. If they find that complaining and whining is not effective, they may try out screaming and yelling. Instead of drawing a hard line, think of how flexible you are willing to be, and then offer that privilege, in reasonable quantities, in the form of a literal "free pass." You can set limits on when the pass can be used, and how often. Your student may not always need it, but will have a way to self-regulate or refresh without having to risk a conflict with you. If they absolutely love debating and arguing with you, you can incorporate that into your lessons through role-play, debates, or other verbal battles.

8. **Do** *be prepared to admit your mistakes:* Many students diagnosed with ODD struggle to give and receive corrective feedback. Instead, they criticize harshly and refuse to take responsibility. Fortunately, if you demonstrate humility (with dignity) you can model better behavior. You can show them how to respond when someone points out a mistake. You can even encourage your students to practice giving corrective feedback by making it into a game, for example, "If you see that I've made a mistake, you can say _____, and I'll check it. If you're right, you get a point! Even though I try not to get it wrong, I like it when you pay close attention."

9. **Do** *use humor, surprise, and storytelling:* You can be serious about teaching and still use humor as a powerful tool in educating your students. Humor is inherently risky because it provokes a reaction that is hard to predict. Your students may chuckle, roll their eyes, stare blankly, or start rolling in the aisles. Humor is also very subjective, but this can be a perfect opportunity to demonstrate perspective-taking and respecting other points of view. Do tell personal stories in the classroom when appropriate. While some students will follow your lead because you are an adult and a "leader" by default, others are more skeptical and do not follow by default. If they need to see you as someone with relevant wisdom and experience, you can tell them stories about how you once learned what they are learning now, what surprised you, what was hard for you, and when it came in handy.

10. **Do** *teach and practice the "positive opposite":* Whenever you ask your students to stop doing something, it's best to make sure they know what they are expected to do instead. But wait! It's easy to give an instruction or make a recommendation, and then walk away as if the job is done. Instead, treat each new behavior as a skill to be learned, and offer opportunities to practice with feedback. A good rule of thumb is "If it's important, teach as if you were training a new employee." Role-play (including playing opposite roles) can help to bridge the gap between theory and practice.

CHAPTER 12

PREPARING TO WRITE AN INDIVIDUALIZED BEHAVIOR PLAN

Individualized behavior plans are a valuable but often misused tool. Their purpose is to:

- Address the underlying reason for behavior that interferes with safety or learning
- Replace the inappropriate behavior with an appropriate behavior that helps the student meet the same need
- Reduce or eliminate the challenging behavior if it continues to pose a threat to safety or compromise learning opportunities.

At their best, individualized behavior plans can pull together valuable ideas from across different disciplines, outline a gradual and thoughtful plan for supporting a student, and guide a consistent and effective strategy that team members can refer to on a daily basis. A good behavior plan will help school staff to practice strategies and prepare materials, using the skills and resources that are already available.

When a behavior plan is created as a formality or as simply another template to fill out, it represents wishful thinking at best, and a waste of time at worst. It does not do any good at all if left to gather dust in a drawer. A behavior plan does not provide an effective intervention if no one remembers what it says or if no one is trained to carry it out. Without planned supports and goals for a struggling student, the goal is simply to hope for the best and "have a good day" as often as possible.

If this is your starting point, keep reading for some simple and effective steps you can take, so that your behavior plan will be specific, effective, and feasible. Your school will probably have its own template for writing an individualized behavior plan, but here are some questions you can answer together with your team before you fill it out. These questions have been laid out as a printable worksheet so that you can explore ideas and collaborate with your administrators, paraprofessionals, and resource teams (see Worksheet 4.1 in Section IV).

Why do we need a behavior plan?

THE TEACHER'S GUIDE TO OPPOSITIONAL DEFIANT DISORDER

As you consider this question, be sure to look at the issue from several different angles, such as:

- Problems you are experiencing as a teacher
- Problems you are observing in the class
- Problems that affect the student's learning and wellbeing.

How does the student describe the problem?

Whether or not the student can state the problem in tactful language, it is important to invite them to explain their perspective, if possible. It is always easier to solve a shared problem in collaboration with a student, so their views are key. If the teacher and the student are not in agreement as to the problem, there are still ways to look for a solution that overlaps and creates a win-win situation.

How does the situation tend to start, and what makes it worse?

Even though challenging behavior may seem to happen suddenly, it does not actually happen "out of nowhere."

- What do you notice when the student is at their best?
- When do you notice things start to "go downhill?" What body language do you see? What statements do you hear? What is happening?
- What do you see when things are at their most intense? What makes it worse at this point? What has been helpful to see you through safely?

What would we like to see more of? What would we like to see less of?

Describe these goals in concrete terms, with the understanding that success will sometimes be achieved gradually, and there are many paths to the same destination. Try to describe what you are seeing now, and what you would like to see. Prioritize goals that benefit the child, while considering the needs of the class as well.

- What do we know about the "why" of this behavior?
- What might the student be moving toward?
- What might the student be moving away from?
- Can we offer this student a better way to meet their needs?

With the understanding that behavior often serves an important purpose, review the steps you have taken to find out what the student needs, what skills might be missing, and how this behavior might be paying off for the student, or indicating an important need that should be met. Consider what you can offer and what the student can be empowered to ask for, in order to meet that need in a healthier way. This new behavior needs to be taught and guided, so a behavior plan should include the steps you will take to:

- Better understand the function, purpose, or relevant variables affecting the challenging behavior
- Select an alternative to "replace" the challenging behavior.

If we could choose just one thing, what would we prioritize?

Although it might be tempting to write a behavior plan that describes a long list of struggles, your time and energy are limited. If you can select a single goal that will benefit your student in a variety of ways, then one effective behavior intervention is better than a handful of ineffective ones.

Can we alter the set-up to make it easier for this student to succeed?

A proactive plan is usually much more effective than a reactive one. After all, your student has a lot of practice making these kinds of mistakes and navigating the chaos that follows, so it's best to start practicing a healthy alternative as soon as possible.

YOUR PLAN FOR FINDING THE "WHY" OF BEHAVIOR

As you read in the section entitled "Finding the 'why' of behavior," there are many different tools available for investigating what needs and desires are hiding behind the challenging behavior you see.

Your school's administrators can advise you about whether your district has a team to help to conduct a formal behavior assessment process such as an FBA. If you do not have support from other team members, you can use some of the tools mentioned in this book to help you begin this step on your own. Any effort you make will be worthwhile, especially when you select tools that fit your school's culture and your own skill set.

When you understand about the context of a particular behavior, you will find yourself less reliant on coercive forms and control, and your interventions will be more helpful.

CREATING A BEHAVIOR PLAN THAT WORKS (AND KEEPS WORKING)

When you have an idea of what your student might be struggling with, and what replacement behaviors might help fill in the gap, you are ready for a practical plan of action. This section is designed to help you write that plan in a way that is feasible and effective.

First of all, here are some incredibly frustrating problems that are common to many behavior plans:

Problem: There are no specific instructions in the behavior plan for when or how to withdraw support. Instead, the supports are provided for as long as the funding is available, which uses up resources unnecessarily. In the meantime, the student habitually leans on those supports instead of developing independent skills.

Problem: The classroom cannot sustain the level of support indicated in the behavior plan due to lack of time or staffing. If the plan gets implemented at all, it is patchy, cobbled-together, and inconsistent.

Problem: The behavior plan does not specify how intense the supports should be, or how long the supports should last, so the supports are offered "whenever possible" but at a level that is too low to make any real difference.

Problem: Even with assistance, the student cannot complete the work assigned, or stay in class for the full length of the class without disruption. This struggle is a source of daily frustration for the student. Despite the supports provided, the student is often faced with a mark of "incomplete" on assignments because the task is too difficult or because they have left the class early.

Problem: The behavior plan includes goals that stay the same from one semester to the next, because no progress has been made. Teachers can try to carry on with strategies even if they seem to be ineffective, or they can quietly set them aside, but there are no opportunities for reassessment mid-year.

Problem: Even though the student is still struggling, they have already progressed past the goals laid out in the behavior plan, so the plan does not contain information or supports that can help them continue to make gains.

A step-by-step framework can help you map out a plan that enables your student to experience more success at every stage. Your aim is to create opportunities for them to learn by practicing the desired behaviors, rather than continuously falling short and suffering the consequences.

You are also helping to set your educational team up for success, because each behavior plan includes specific *levels* of support (high, medium, low) using measurable indicators to signal when to move from one level to the next. In this way, your team can invest time and energy into ambitious behavior plans, knowing that the strategy will be temporary, not indefinite.

This type of plan has three key features:

- Specific goals, laid out like stepping stones, that keep success within reach
- Close attention to progress so milestones can be celebrated, and adjustments can be made in case progress is stalled
- Support that sets the student up for success and avoids escalating disciplinary procedures or power struggles.

These plans are *graduated*, meaning that they are mapped out in small steps, so that you can gradually shift your expectations and withdraw support as the student builds independence.

- Step-by-step support plan (Type 1): Students who need extra help but who successfully meet school expectations (with the right support).
- Step-by-step modified expectations plan (Type 2): Students who need modifications to school expectations as they build skills.
- Step-by-step transition plan (Type 3): Students who struggle most in between tasks, and need help with transitions.

STEP-BY-STEP SUPPORT PLAN (TYPE 1)

One type of graduated behavior plan involves offering a lot of help to ensure success at first, then scaling back when the student is ready. Ideally, this can set them up *to experience success more often.* The criteria for success do not change much, but the level of independence gradually increases.

Level of support	Type of available support	What will success look like?
High	<ul><li>Visual prompts</li><li>Partner working side-by-side</li><li>Frequent positive feedback</li><li>Close physical proximity, supervision</li></ul>	The student meets the classroom expectations with significant help and preparation.
Medium	<ul><li>Daily check-ins and follow-ups</li><li>Checklist for self-monitoring</li><li>Visual prompts</li><li>Hand signals</li><li>Plans and routines</li><li>Prepared back-up plans</li></ul>	The student meets the classroom expectations with proactive strategies to prepare and cues to redirect.
Low	<ul><li>Weekly check-ins</li><li>Student asks for help when needed</li></ul>	The student meets the classroom expectations alongside typical peers.

STEP-BY-STEP MODIFIED EXPECTATIONS PLAN (TYPE 2)

Another type of graduated behavior plan ensures success by modifying the expectations so that they are appropriate based on the student's current skill set, with the focus on building those skills and extending the expectations accordingly.

Level of modification	Types of available modifications	What will success look like?
High	• Tasks broken down into smaller steps • Tasks presented with photos or visuals • Frequent breaks • Movement and sensory breaks • Supplements to aid memory • Instructions presented in writing, checklists, illustrations, repetition • Alternative materials such as manipulatives, flashcards, illustrations • Alternative format such as participation in games, typing on keyboard, drawings, verbal responses • Works on tasks in preferred location • Student starts task independently, finishes with assistance • Student starts with assistance, finishes independently	The student begins to meet the school's expectation.
Medium	• Confirming that instructions are understood • Offering choice of format • Task is presented as a short list of steps • Limited number of breaks offered • Other modifications when requested by student	The student meets some of the school's expectations.
Low	• Instructions are given with class • Class-wide strategies for improving cooperation	The student meets most or all of the school's expectations.

STEP-BY-STEP TRANSITION PLAN (TYPE 3)

For many students, the most difficult time of the day occurs between activities. They often struggle to stop a preferred activity, switch their attention to a new task, or get started on a difficult job. If your biggest source of conflict happens between activities, here are some options for offering support.

Level of modification	Types of available support for transitions	What will success look like?
High	• Several alerts to prepare for transition • Transition broken down into steps • Regular positive feedback during transitions • Visual timer • Extra time to reach agreed milestone before transition • Proximity to trusted adult during transitions • Daily visual schedule reviewed with student • Practice, role-play transitions • Verbally repeat steps between tasks	The student will be able to transition between activities, with support, and some additional time.
Medium	• One or two alerts to prepare for transition • Visual schedule available when needed • Positive feedback on completion of successful transition • Extra time available on request	The student successfully transitions between activities, with preparation and occasional support when needed.
Low	• Instructions for transitions are given with class • Student is empowered to independently use other strategies when needed (visual schedule, timer) • Class-wide strategies for improving cooperation	The student will be able to complete transition alongside peers, without extra support.

MEASUREMENT AND FEEDBACK

Without planned supports and goals, we cannot measure to see whether our efforts are making any difference, and we do not know if the student is better off at the end of the year aside from some general impressions and recollections.

Describing practical and attainable goals

Setting goals can be tricky because we know what we would like to see, but how do we get there? Most teachers would like their students to be more compliant, less aggressive, and more respectful to others, but how do we define that? Teachers are often encouraged to use SMART goals, which end up looking like a combination of wishful thinking and fractions. Here is an example of some goals you might see on a typical behavior plan:

Behavior	Target frequency
The student will cooperate with teacher instructions	8 times out of 10 opportunities
The student will exit for recess without hitting peers	8 times out of 10 opportunities

Unfortunately, this description does not suggest a clear way forward. If the student is currently succeeding only 2 out of 10 times, what is the strategy that will help them improve? If there is no progress halfway through the year, does the plan change? What reminders, supports, and cues can improve the chances of success? How long will these supports be in place?

If possible, think of the steps you will take along the way, and try to be specific. What would those degrees of success look like? (In other words, shoot for the stars, but bring a ladder.)

When you choose to monitor progress frequently, this will benefit you and your student in several ways. You gain the opportunity to:

- Evaluate whether the supports and modifications have been effective
- Adjust the supports and modifications if they are not effective
- Celebrate with and encourage your student
- Ask them what is working well
- Move from more intense to less intense intervention, and offer more independence to them.

Your student gains the opportunity to:

- Review and celebrate progress
- Set personal goals
- Tell you about how the plan is working
- Make suggestions to adjust the plan if needed.

What will you measure?

Once you have decided to measure your progress, you will quickly be confronted with a multitude of decisions. Here are some principles to bear in mind:

1. Your behavior goal should be *easy to interpret*. Any observer should be able to come to the same conclusion about whether the goal was met or not. Avoid language that could be interpreted differently by different people, such as "speaking nicely" or "working hard."
2. Your behavior goal should be *simple to track*. Here are some useful options:

a. You can measure events as a whole (e.g., completes worksheet, hangs up jacket, swears at teacher).

b. You can measure quantities (e.g., minutes spent at desk or time before starting task).

c. You can set a standard, and record whether it is met (e.g., comes in from recess before 10 o'clock or completes work assigned before end of class).

3. Tracking is *not a long-term project*, but a tool to be used with a purpose. When you commit to tracking for a short period of time and then evaluating your results, it is easier to make that extra effort. Once you have collected information for a week or two, you can decide whether:

a. Your student is ready to meet school expectations with less support or fewer modifications.

b. They are still struggling, and changes should be made to supports or modifications.

c. They are improving but not ready to progress.

d. The information is incomplete, and tracking should continue.

4. Your behavior goal should be *revisited regularly*. Schedule meetings in your calendar or set reminders to make sure progress is underway or changes can be made.

5. Your behavior information should be collected in a way that is *easy to read*. Here are some examples of visual displays of information that you can fill in quickly, or ask your student to fill in for you.

Tracking sheet: Example 1

Asked permission before leaving the classroom:				
Monday	Tuesday	Wednesday	Thursday	Friday
+	–	+	+	–

Tracking sheet: Example 2

Minutes seated at desk	Monday	Tuesday	Wednesday	Thursday	Friday
25					
20			X		X
15			X	X	X
10		X	X	X	X
5	X	X	X	X	X

Tracking sheet: Example 3

Date:	My daily goals	Circle the answer
	I sat in my own space on the carpet today.	Yes/No
	I took a break when I started to get frustrated.	Yes/No
	I politely told my friends when I needed personal space.	Yes/No
		Yes/No

cont.

		Yes/No
		Yes/No
		Yes/No
		Yes/No

Other ways to track behavior

Your days are undoubtedly busy, and your desk might already be full, but there are quick and creative ways to take note of the information that is important to you. If it is not feasible to use a pen and paper, other convenient and inexpensive options are available, including:

- Tally counters
- Beads on a string (try an online search for the term "tagulator" to find tutorials to make your own)
- Abacus
- Smartphone apps
- Kitchen timers, egg timers.

A PLAN FOR EVERY KIND OF DAY

A behavior plan is not just for moments of crisis; a really effective behavior plan will:

- Reinforce what works, leading to more "good days"
- Identify quick and effective strategies to reset and regulate
- Prepare a safety plan for the most difficult days.

You can use the colors of a traffic light to help you remember the three types of strategies you can include in a behavior plan.

Green: positive and proactive strategies

A green light in a traffic signal means it is safe to go ahead.

The *green* part of the plan is all about setting your student up for success. These are everyday, preventative supports that help your students meet basic needs, nurture a sense of safety, and build positive personal connections. Green strategies do not have to rely on advanced knowledge or expertise. They can be as simple as a friendly greeting in the morning, a few extra pencils in your top desk drawer, or a visual cue to remind your student to take a break when needed. Green strategies can also be based on your student's strengths, so you can encourage them to use existing skills and interests in areas where they are not as comfortable.

Green strategies are best used when everything is "all clear," to make sure things continue to go well. If your student is having "good days" or even "good moments," then why not make the most of them? Green strategies build on what already works, and they empower students to get what they need. Positive and proactive strategies are often overlooked in favor of reactive measures or benign neglect, but if you are at the stage where you need a behavior plan, make sure to consider using some (not all!) green strategies.

Everyone on the team can help with green strategies. For example, if breakfast is an important precursor for "good days," parents can help by providing food in the morning (and sending extra snacks for emergency back-up use). A quick conversation with the outdoor supervisor during recess time can help a student to choose a group of friends to play with, or find the right equipment before a fight breaks out.

Think of cues that might help start things in a positive way:

- Would a daily reminder or visual schedule help?
- Is it possible to plan check-ins with your student so you can touch base before a little struggle turns into a major crisis?
- Can you practice this positive behavior together so both of you know what it will look like?
- What would remind you to point out the positives more often?
- When students are calm and happy, they are in the best possible state to learn new skills and be creative, so green strategies include role-playing and generating possible solutions.

Green strategies are preventative, so they can be used to teach students how to ask for what they need, or get access to what they want, in a positive and healthy way; they set your students up for success, reducing anxiety and unexpected surprises, so they will also include back-up plans and visual schedules.

Potential green strategies to include in your student's individualized behavior plan:

- Boost motivation by tracking progress and seeing growth
- Boost motivation by offering choice
- Boost motivation by tapping into values and a sense of belonging
- Provide sensory tools
- Practice positive opposites
- Role-play together to explore different solutions to common problems
- Imagine many possible solutions together
- Create and practice back-up plans
- Highlight opportunities to practice flexibility
- Use stories and ask questions to teach perspective-taking
- Remind students of ways to ask for what they need
- Create visual schedules together
- Break difficult transitions into easier mini-routines
- Check-in with student to assess needs; celebrate success

- Teach self-monitoring strategies
- Capture important reminders with posters; step-by-step instructions
- Plan movement breaks
- Schedule mindful moments
- Invite peer mentors to help out and join in
- Train teachers and support team to use declarative language
- Use timers and previews proactively.

Yellow: sensitive strategies to adjust and redirect
When you see a yellow light on the traffic signal, proceed with caution.

Yellow strategies can be deployed at the first sign of trouble. Often, you will be able to detect small signs of distraction, distress, or withdrawal prior to a major outburst, so a plan will set you up to respond promptly and effectively.

Yellow strategies are best used when you start to see a warning sign or a known stress trigger; they are calming and redirecting. If you know what kind of situations usually trigger stress, conflict, or confusion, then a yellow plan will help your student cope with whatever cannot be avoided or prevented. For example, you can set up a separate area for self-regulation, collect a basket of sensory tools to use when they are frustrated, or arrange a signal to remind them of the plans you made together.

If you watch carefully, there are often nonverbal signs that your student is starting to struggle. These signs will vary depending on the student, but there is often a consistent pattern that you will learn over time. When you have detected these early signs, then a raised voice, deep sighs, or lips pressed together will remind you to put the yellow plan into action.

Your student can use them independently to self-regulate, or you can invite them to utilize them when needed.

Some yellow strategies need preparation ahead of time so they can be deployed at a moment's notice:

- A *prearranged* break pass
- Access to snacks
- Access to water
- Access to fidgets
- Calming space
- Use of sensory tools
- Movement breaks
- Extra time
- Mindful moments
- Back-up plans
- Timers
- Prearranged cues for breaks
- Breathing techniques
- Change of scenery
- Offer a chance to back up and try again
- Invite negotiation
- Encourage self-advocacy
- Emotional validation
- Offer a rationale.

Red: safety and recovery

When you see a red light on a traffic signal, stop. It is not safe to proceed.

There will be days when you are called to help with a student who has already spiraled into a state of intense distress. A bad night's sleep or a tense argument on the morning school bus can wear down your student's patience quickly, so "the straw that breaks the camel's back" could be your first conversation of the day.

The *red* plan does not prevent problems or solve them. It simply helps everyone cope with a state of crisis, with minimal damage. Many schools make the mistake of preparing a "safety plan" for when things are at their worst, but do not have many strategies for making sure this plan is not needed in the first place.

The first priority of the red plan is safety. Very often, well-meaning adults make the mistake of offering reason, logic, ethics, problem-solving, or advice to a situation that is so heated that it all simply melts into emotional lava. A student in crisis will often trigger a sense of danger in everyone else, so screaming, throwing objects, ripping papers, and running away will drag others along into the crisis too. The assurance of security is what they need most, and if you can establish a safe place for your student to self-regulate, you will find your way through together.

Similarly, red strategies can be used when you and your student are on the path to an unavoidable headlong collision. The purpose of a red strategy is to avoid catastrophe and to speed up recovery when the green and yellow plans have failed. These plans are not teaching plans; red plans are for coping and safety.

Here are some factors that you can consider as you create your red plan:

Location: Where does your student feel safest? Often, a student in crisis is further triggered by others who are staring, laughing, or giving orders. A space that is contained is helpful, but it is best not to create a sense of confinement such as a locked door or a dead end.

Body language: Your nonverbal communication speaks volumes. If you can reach eye level with your student, this often helps lower the emotional temperature. Be aware of your posture. Facing your student directly may be interpreted as confrontational, but if you adjust your footing you can communicate support without triggering more anxiety.

Students in need of a red plan are:

- Becoming aggressive toward others
- In danger of hurting themselves
- Overwhelmed with emotion
- Destroying property; in a rage
- Attempting to run away from supervision
- Making credible threats.

In past years, you may have been trained to use strategies such as "escape extinction" and "following through" when students are extremely agitated and refusing to follow instructions. The purpose of these strategies was ostensibly to make sure that the consequences of the maladaptive behavior were appropriate for learning. For instance, if a student screamed and hid in the closet when asked to work on a handwriting task, a teacher using "escape extinction" would ensure that the student was not allowed to avoid the task, otherwise the consequence of the maladaptive behavior might provide an escape, and would therefore "reinforce" the maladaptive behavior. Similarly, when teachers are advised to "follow through" after giving a command, students who refuse would eventually have to complete the task. If the student does not comply immediately, then, as part of the "escape extinction" procedure, the teacher would ignore further protests, and withhold other kinds of preferred activities until the task is complete.

This kind of rigid response is not recommended as part of your red plan for a number of reasons:

- When students are unable to refuse, they may escalate their behavior, and become more aggressive or anxious. This could put you, your student, or others, in danger.
- "Escape extinction" does not consider a student's right to refuse, and it does not respect their dignity.
- Students diagnosed with ODD already have experience resisting demands and may be willing to hold out much longer than you would like, or go to dangerous lengths to avoid giving in.
- Empathy and negotiation are valuable skills for students diagnosed with ODD, so they should be modeled by caring adults, in lieu of coercion.
- Students refuse and fail to comply frequently throughout the day, but "escape extinction" is usually reserved for students who protest loudly and vehemently. This puts students who struggle with emotional dysregulation at an unfair disadvantage.
- When a student is in crisis, they are not primed for learning cause-and-effect. Attempts at "teaching a lesson" often fail because students are already preoccupied with the stressful experience they are having.
- Students who experience control tactics may feel a sense of helplessness, a common feature of traumatic experiences, which will damage their trust in you.
- "Escape extinction" does not teach replacement skills such as negotiating, flexible alternatives, or self-advocacy. The only goal of "escape extinction" is compliance.
- "Escape extinction" does not help to explain why a student is refusing, so it does not solve problems such as anxiety, pain, or confusion.

If you are running into a lot of refusal, resist the temptation to resort to controlling systems immediately. Try to understand the reason for the refusal, and the need behind it. Offer alternatives, and teach socially effective forms of refusal and negotiation as part of your green and yellow plans.

Red strategies that prioritize safety and de-escalation:

- Provide physical safety, space, and time
- Minimize talking; avoid giving commands
- Offer sensory experiences that reinforce a sense of safety, such as lights, blanket, shelter, privacy, and pressure
- Offer emotional support and a listening ear
- Process, reason, and problem-solve only when the student is ready
- Nonverbal communication is crucial to signaling safety
- Allow distractions to be a part of de-escalation, such as reading or music
- Repetitive activities like cleaning or throwing can be soothing.

Responding to emotional dysregulated children in moments of crisis

While a typical child might be able to problem-solve and use logic while also processing strong emotions, children diagnosed with ODD should not be expected to do so. In an escalated emotional state, these children are even less amenable to reason than usual. Use of "logical consequences" and explanations may pass them by completely, or backfire in unpleasant ways. Instead, consider addressing your priorities one step at a time, instead of all at once.

1. PHYSICAL SAFETY

Your first priority will be practical: ensure safety and facilitate physical self-regulation. Allow time and space for the child's body to self-regulate. Communicate in a way that makes sure everyone feels safe. While it is tempting to use warnings and an angry tone of voice, this increases the risk that an emotionally dysregulated student will continue to feel "threatened." Gently guide people into areas where they will not be harmed.

2. EMOTIONAL SUPPORT

Without the threat of imminent danger, real or perceived, your student may not be ready to solve difficult problems yet, but the possibility for emotional self-regulation is starting to improve. Your presence, your willingness to listen, your acceptance, and your calm are enough for now. Resist the urge to teach and advise too soon (often people need to "feel heard" before they can start to listen).

3. PROBLEM-SOLVING AND REASON

When a sense of security and connection has been restored, your student will be in a better position to think logically, understand the perspectives of others, and get back on track.

PART IV

WORSHEETS

This section is all about learning by *doing*. The activities can be completed on your own, but they can also be used in groups and workshops to cover all the material in this book in a single event. *The access code to download these worksheets is SBPTLHN.*

As you complete these activities, you will get a chance to examine your own beliefs and experiences about challenging behavior and ODD. You will also find practical tools that you can bring with you into your next team meeting, to dig deep and find the insights you need to make a real difference in the lives of your students diagnosed with ODD.

1.1 OPPOSITIONAL DEFIANT DISORDER: THE VIEW FROM THE OUTSIDE

A diagnosis of ODD describes only the behavior we can see on the outside.

1. What do people *see* when they look at a child diagnosed with ODD? What kinds of behaviors do they observe? Fill in the blanks on the outside of the circle.
   (Example: argues with adults, stubborn, difficult, cries easily)

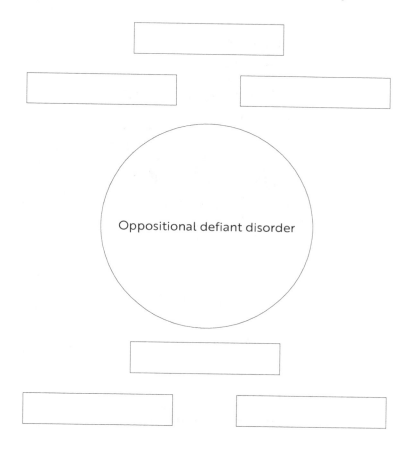

2. What else do people tend to *assume* about students diagnosed with ODD? Add these to the outside of the circle.
   (Example: spoiled, entitled, manipulative, unstable)

Generalizations, stereotypes, and assumptions leave many students misunderstood and unsupported. As you go further into this book, you will learn more about what might be going on beneath the surface for individual students with challenging behavior.

For now, let us leave the inside of the circle empty, as a reminder that we do not always know what is happening on the "inside" when we meet a student who exhibits difficult and defiant behavior.

1.2 YOUR EXPERIENCE WITH "OPPOSITIONAL" AND "DEFIANT" STUDENTS

Unless you have been very lucky or you are just starting out as a teacher, you have probably met at least one student who fits the description of "oppositional" and "defiant."

Reflection questions

What emotions come up for you when you are confronted with oppositional and defiant behavior?	
Can you think of a student who was, frankly speaking, hard to like at first?	
Did you discover anything about this student that made it easier to like them?	

1.3 SPECIFIC STRUGGLES AND STRENGTHS ASSESSMENT

As you have seen, students diagnosed with oppositional defiant disorder (ODD) may display similar challenging behaviors, but they often experience the world very differently. Try to bring to mind a particular child for the purpose of this exercise.

This worksheet will help to identify areas of strength and struggle for that individual student. Most students diagnosed with ODD will be on the lower end of some of these rating scales, but you will find that two children with similar problems at school can score very differently when you look a little bit closer.

Emotional regulation

1. Cries easily, yells, or swears regardless of who is around.
2. Usually in a bad mood.
3. Typical ups and downs.
4. Surprisingly calm, even when challenged.

Executive functioning skills

1. Very easy to distract; extremely inflexible.
2. Somewhat disorganized; impulsive; a bit forgetful.
3. Can usually follow classroom routines, when motivated.
4. Plans ahead; follows through; good with details.

Communication and verbal problem-solving

1. Tends to make threats and give orders; doesn't negotiate well.
2. Limited ability to share ideas and understand perspective.
3. Conversations go well when they are calm.
4. Can debate easily.

Academic abilities

1. Needs repetition and many examples to learn new ideas.
2. Can complete schoolwork with frequent help and simplification.
3. Completes schoolwork without much additional support (when motivated).
4. High scores on tests of verbal and visual reasoning.

Social skills

1. Hard to like; struggles to be polite.
2. Makes friends but doesn't always keep them long.
3. Has friends; occasional tension, but can see other points of view.
4. Charming and persuasive.

Motivation

1. Very limited interests and attention span.
2. Gives up quickly; prefers easy activities.
3. Can wait without too much frustration; focus for short periods.
4. Stays on-task; single-minded and determined.

When you look at this profile, remember that your students have strengths that help to balance out some of the weaker areas. This profile will help you predict what kind of activities will be most successful with your student, and which activities require support or accommodation.

1.4 EMOTIONAL SELF-REGULATION

Emotional regulation is a complex process that involves our bodies, our experiences, our thoughts, our physical responses, our genes, our expectations, and so on, and there are many possible reasons for an emotional struggle.

Think of a student who has been emotionally dysregulated lately. Using this framework, write down any ideas you have for understanding that response in context.

Stressful environments and Adverse Childhood Events (ACE) What circumstances, events or past traumas might be adding stress?	
Physiological changes; difficulty recovering from stress Is your student extra-vulnerable to stress for some reason (sensory processing issues, grief, physical pain, etc.)? Are there any genetic or developmental differences that could affect your student's emotional responses? Does your student have difficulty predicting what will happen next?	
Cognitive vulnerabilities and executive functioning skills Does your student have difficulty predicting what will happen next? How does your student "talk to themselves" in difficult moments?	

Lack of social support What kind of social support is available to your student? How do others respond when they need help? Does your student share important beliefs and values with the people around them? Does your student understand social cues or do they struggle to make sense of them?	
Limited behavioral repertoire How do others respond when your student becomes very upset? When is your student most successful at recruiting help or resolving problems? Do other people respond when they self-advocate?	

You can use the results of this assessment with the next activity to help you choose activities that will be successful for your student.

1.5 ACTIVITIES FOR STRENGTHS AND STRUGGLES

This profile will help you predict what kind of activities will be most successful with your student, and which activities require support or accommodation, based on the specific struggles outlined in Worksheet 1.3, the **Specific struggles and strengths assessment**.

Emotional self-regulation

If your student struggles with emotional self-regulation, certain kinds of activities may be challenging, especially where there is the potential for disappointment, uncertainty, or loss.

Common triggers:

- Competitive games
- Group projects
- Unexpected changes to the schedule.

Key supports:

- Practicing flexibility
- Planning alternative solutions
- Using coping statements and positive self-talk
- Facilitate asking for a break.

Executive functioning skills

If your student struggles with executive functioning skills, tasks that require memory, planning, impulse control, and organization are especially difficult.

Common triggers:

- Getting started
- Narrowing down many options
- Remembering detailed instructions
- Time limits.

Key supports:

- Access to written instructions, illustrations, or photos
- Help finding a starting point
- Setting mini-deadlines
- Removing distractions
- Options for sensory self-regulation.

Communication and verbal problem-solving

If your student struggles with communication and verbal problem-solving, activities that require quick replies and negotiation (especially with peers) will be particularly difficult.

Common triggers:

- Written assignments
- Cooperative tasks with peers
- Role-play.

Key supports:

- Multiple-choice options to choose from
- Extra time for processing
- Pre-written messages
- Scribing.

Academics

If your student struggles with academics in one or more areas, further assessment is needed to check for specific learning disabilities, such as dyslexia or dysgraphia. Screening should also include sensory processing issues and mental health issues such as anxiety, because stress in these areas can interfere with attention and participation.

Common triggers:

- Tests
- Report cards
- Assessments that will rank the student among peers.

Key supports:

- Testing and screening for learning disabilities
- Alternative materials for learning such as manipulatives, games, role-play, illustrations, and video
- Alternative methods for evaluation, such as demonstrations, drawing, and computer presentations (depending on specific skills and needs).

Social skills

If your student struggles with social skills, activities that require some teamwork and perspective-taking will be challenging (but worthwhile). Look out for emotional dysregulation as a possible barrier, as a social disconnection can be a stress trigger, and also contribute to further alienation and misunderstanding.

Common triggers:

- Unstructured time
- Sharing space and materials
- Cooperative group projects.

Key supports:

- Scripts for students to support interactions
- Role-play to practice challenging moments
- Preparation and rehearsal with your student to side-step known problems, such as how to change the subject and how to respond when a suggestion is declined.

Motivation

If your student struggles with motivation, they may benefit from an assessment that can determine if there are any conditions that affect focus and attention, such as attention deficit disorder. However, emotional dysregulation can certainly have an impact on motivation. If your student is quite anxious, it may be hard for them to embrace new challenges or risk making mistakes.

Common triggers:

- Independent work
- Open-ended projects
- Repetitive, lengthy tasks.

Key supports:

- Visuals that track progress toward a goal
- Games, to add novelty and interaction
- Online quizzes for quick feedback and error correction
- Mental health check-ins; growth mindset feedback.

1.6 STRUGGLES–STRENGTHS WORKSHEET

When you focus on your students' strengths and abilities, you can spend more time setting up opportunities for them to succeed, encouraging them when they are successful.

Knowing that struggles and strengths can sometimes be connected, like two sides of the same coin, and with the understanding that it is often easier to spot a struggle than a strength, here are some common struggles associated with a diagnosis of oppositional defiant disorder (ODD). For each struggle, try to come up with a corresponding strength:

A child who is considered...	...can have hidden strengths, such as...
• Impulsive • Pushy • Blunt • Uncompromising • Easily upset • Rude • Rigid • Rebellious • Defiant • Argumentative • Aggressive • Single-minded • Sneaky	

STRENGTHS

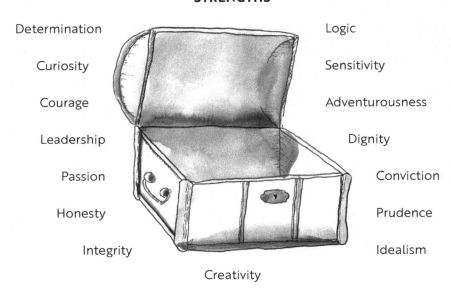

Determination   Logic

Curiosity   Sensitivity

Courage   Adventurousness

Leadership   Dignity

Passion   Conviction

Honesty   Prudence

Integrity   Idealism

Creativity

2.1 AUTONOMY-SUPPORTING SELF-ASSESSMENT

How autonomy supporting is your classroom? Consider these qualities of an autonomy-supporting classroom and check off the descriptions that match your priorities:

	I invite students to share their perspectives.
	I make it a point to find out what my students care about.
	I choose activities that pique curiosity.
	The emotional wellbeing of students is important to me.
	I adapt my teaching style to the mood of my students.
	I match my learning goals to what my students care about.
	I explain why something is important before I ask my students to do it.
	I help my students see how far they have come.
	I try to make sure my classroom as a safe place where students can belong.
	I encourage my students to set goals and track their progress.
	I frequently offer choices in my class.
	When my students express disapproval or discomfort, I'm open to listening.
	I try not to give commands or pressure my students to obey.
	I try to see the class from my students' point of view.
	I demonstrate a lot of patience.

2.2 BUILDING RAPPORT: BEING WARM

Compliance can be achieved when you apply pressure, but co-operation is freely given.

To establish a safe, caring environment where your students are willing to follow your lead, you will keep coming back to the building blocks of rapport-building:

– Being warm
– Being attentive
– Being responsive.

Genuine warmth and interest in your students is such a valuable quality. Your ability to bring warmth can result in academic boosts for your students (Hamre & Pianta 2005), and will often help to decrease rates of disruptive behavior in the classroom, but it does not always come effortlessly. Your personal approach might be lively or gentle; it might be soothing or invigorating; but it is uniquely yours. It grows out of your ability to bring optimism, joy, and connection to unexpected moments.

Place a checkmark beside the practices you would like to try to introduce into your classroom. (To help you stay consistent, you can even write some ideas into your monthly planner so you will have fresh ideas in the weeks to come.)

Nurture optimism

☐ Share a story with your students of a time you struggled to learn something, and how you figured it out.

☐ Think of an excellent teacher you have had. Remember the impact of those little moments, and commit to carrying on that legacy.

☐ Use a visual display to show how your students' efforts add up to big results over time.

☐ Highlight stories of people in your community who have stepped up to help others. Find out what skills they needed to make a positive change.

☐ Ask your students to share something they are "surprisingly good at."

☐ Remind yourself of how little your students once were, and how they are still a work in progress.

☐ Treat disagreements as an opportunity to listen and learn about each other's point of view.

☐ Remember that little efforts can have a big ripple effect.

Invite joy

- ☐ Introduce your students to things that light you up, such as your passion for gardening, your favorite song, or photos of your pet.
- ☐ What mood would you like to set in the classroom? Choose a song that matches that mood (e.g., gentle, calm, upbeat, determined) and use it as your "entrance" music for a day.
- ☐ If you have a projector or a screen in your classroom, show some of your favorite works of art. You can just enjoy the beauty, or spark a conversation on the historical and social context of the piece.
- ☐ Once in a while, challenge your students to respond in an unexpected way. This could include writing their answers on paper airplanes and throwing them, speaking in a code language, only walking backwards, or charades. Any kind of break from the regular routine is a chance to laugh and refresh.

Cultivate a class culture

- ☐ It's hard to feel safe if we don't feel that we belong. Remind your students that in your classroom, acceptance does not have to be earned.
- ☐ Rituals and routines are comforting and they help to establish what sets your classroom apart.
- ☐ How do you welcome your students? What do you want them to know when they come in?
- ☐ How do you close your lessons when time is up? What do you want students to remember when they leave?
- ☐ Teach your students how to recognize and celebrate each other's strengths. Provide opportunities for your students to give each other feedback. Use a template or fill-in-the-blank structure to give examples as they begin to notice and encourage each other.

2.3 BUILDING RAPPORT: BEING ATTENTIVE

The purpose of these activities is to help you learn more about your students, but also to remind them that they are noticed and valued.

Place a checkmark beside the practices you would like to try to introduce into your classroom. (To help you stay consistent, you can even write some ideas into your monthly planner so you will have fresh ideas in the weeks to come.)

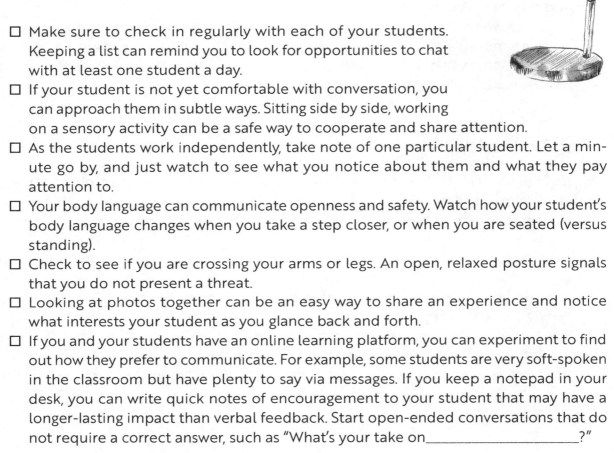

☐ Make sure to check in regularly with each of your students. Keeping a list can remind you to look for opportunities to chat with at least one student a day.

☐ If your student is not yet comfortable with conversation, you can approach them in subtle ways. Sitting side by side, working on a sensory activity can be a safe way to cooperate and share attention.

☐ As the students work independently, take note of one particular student. Let a minute go by, and just watch to see what you notice about them and what they pay attention to.

☐ Your body language can communicate openness and safety. Watch how your student's body language changes when you take a step closer, or when you are seated (versus standing).

☐ Check to see if you are crossing your arms or legs. An open, relaxed posture signals that you do not present a threat.

☐ Looking at photos together can be an easy way to share an experience and notice what interests your student as you glance back and forth.

☐ If you and your students have an online learning platform, you can experiment to find out how they prefer to communicate. For example, some students are very soft-spoken in the classroom but have plenty to say via messages. If you keep a notepad in your desk, you can write quick notes of encouragement to your student that may have a longer-lasting impact than verbal feedback. Start open-ended conversations that do not require a correct answer, such as "What's your take on_____?"

2.4 BUILDING RAPPORT: BEING RESPONSIVE

When you are responsive to your students, they understand that their input matters and their needs will be respected.

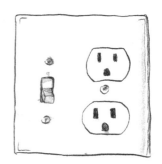

Even in a large group setting, there are so many opportunities to check in with your students and let them make individual decisions. Choices do not have to put your student on the spot or require anything in exchange. They can simply be a demonstration of thoughtfulness and consideration:

- Would you like the door open or closed?
- Should we start with creative writing or small group reading today?
- Would you like to take a break after we finish this?
- Do you prefer to read at your desk or at the table?

Your students sometimes state their needs and preferences without saying a word, so another type of responsiveness is nonverbal. Examples of nonverbal responsiveness include:

- Checking to see if students have finished working before starting a transition
- Noticing expressions of interest and surprise; adjusting lessons when curiosity is sparked or in response to a student's question
- Increasing energy and pace when students look tired or disengaged
- Sitting quietly near a student who seems distressed; checking to see if they turn toward you or turn away.

Use this space to jot down the ideas that occur to you, as you focus on adding choice and responsiveness to your daily teaching practice.

Question 1. What choices can you offer in your classroom?

....

....

....

Question 2. What small changes do you want to be more alert to?

....

....

....

2.5 MOTIVATION AND MEANING

According to the theory of self-determination (Deci and Ryan), people are motivated to take part in activities that offer:

- Meaningful choice
- Growth and progress
- Belonging and relatedness.

People invest time and money on their hobbies for the sheer enjoyment of it. When you look at this list of common hobbies, can you see how they might offer meaningful choice, growth, and progress, or belonging and relatedness?

Meaningful choice	Growth and progress	Belonging and relatedness

Jogging
Knitting
Cooking
Photography
Board games

Video games
Painting
Golf
Yoga
Sewing

Baking
Gardening
Hiking

What are your hobbies? What motivates you most:

- Meaningful choice?
- Growth and progress?
- Belonging and relatedness?

3.1 SEARCHING FOR THE "WHY" OF BEHAVIOR

There is no single answer to the question of why we do what we do, but it's important to *stay curious*. Instead of looking for a disorder or a trait to explain behavior, this exercise will help you look for possibilities. Read the scenario and write down at least one guess.

Problem behavior from your point of view	What's the problem from the child's point of view?
1. You ask Louis to take out his math book and answer the first questions. He looks away and does not respond.	
2. Class is not over yet, but Colleen has already packed up her books and started walking quietly toward the door.	
3. As you read a story to the class, Zachary takes a toy out of his pocket and waves it at a friend. You call his name, and he rolls his eyes but does not put the toy away.	
4. You return to class after the lunch break and find Yevgenia standing at the front of the room, writing obscene words on the blackboard.	
5. It's time for the weekly spelling test, so you place a sheet of paper on each desk. Natalia immediately starts peeling pieces from the edge of the paper and rolling them up in her fingers.	
6. Every recess, Damien claims the ball and refuses to share it with his classmates. This morning, one of them complained, so he bounced it off his classmate's head.	
7. You discover that your drawer of rewards is open, and realize that Shoshana is holding a handful, passing them to her best friends.	
8. Ju Kwan has been coming in from recess in a bad mood lately. You approach him to ask what's wrong, and he calls you a surprisingly vulgar name.	

3.2 UNDERSTANDING BEHAVIOR

Read the scenarios and write down at least one guess.

Scenario	What could the student be moving toward?	What could the student be moving away from?	Source of stress? Missing skill?
1. You ask Louis to take out his math book and answer the first questions. He looks away and does not respond.			
2. Class is not over yet, but Colleen has already packed up her books and started walking quietly toward the door.			
3. As you read a story to the class, Zachary takes a toy out of his pocket and waves it at a friend. You call his name, and he rolls his eyes but does not put the toy away.			
4. You return to class after the lunch break and find Yevgenia standing at the front of the room, writing obscene words on the blackboard.			

5. It's time for the weekly spelling test, so you place a sheet of paper on each desk. Natalia immediately starts peeling pieces from the edge of the paper and rolling them up in her fingers.			
6. Every recess, Damien claims the ball and refuses to share it with his classmates. This morning, one of them complained, so he bounced it off his classmate's head.			
7. You discover that your drawer of rewards is open, and realize that Shoshana is holding a handful, passing them to her best friends.			
8. Ju Kwan has been coming in from recess in a bad mood lately. You approach him to ask what's wrong, and he calls you a surprisingly vulgar name.			

157

3.3 REPLACEMENT BEHAVIORS

If you are trying to minimize disruptive or dangerous behaviors in your classroom, it's best to start by assuming that the behavior meets a need or communicates something important. Ideally, your student will be able to express that need in a way that does not violate the rights of other people in the classroom, but for now, there is a conflict and something needs to change.

What could take the place of the "problem behavior"? There are many possible answers, but the table below outlines two paths you can take on your search. Consider the situations shown in the table from your point of view, and the point of view of your student. Is there a solution that meets everyone's needs?

	What is the expected, proper way of behaving in that moment? Can you state it in positive terms?	Does the "problem behavior" actually solve a problem for the student? If so, what would be another option for solving this problem in a healthier way?
Munazza does not follow the morning routine. She comes in late, drops her jacket on the floor, and says she cannot find her pencil and books. Without help from an adult, she often misses most of the first activity of the day.		
Roland does not raise his hand to answer questions in class, but when the teacher calls on him, he seems to enjoy giving ridiculous answers to the questions. Sometimes his classmates laugh, and sometimes there is uncomfortable silence.		

3.4 ADDING VALUE AND SATISFACTION
TO THE SCHOOL EXPERIENCE

Researchers studying student engagement and willingness (see, for example, Reeve *et al.* 2004) have found that teachers can improve their students' everyday learning experience with the following practices:

- Listening to students' opinions and concerns
- Making time for independent work
- Recognizing improvement and mastery
- Offering progress-enabling hints when students seem stuck
- Responding to comments and questions
- Acknowledging student perspectives.

Pulling together everything you have learned about motivation so far...

	Boosting suspense, wonder, curiosity, and humor	Offering feedback and recognition	Tracking own progress	Meaningful choice, connecting to values
Give yourself a pat on the shoulder for everything you are already doing!				
Where do you see opportunities to add these practices?				

4.1 BEHAVIOR PLAN: TEAM PRIORITY WORKSHEET

Purpose of behavior plan	
Specific behavior to decrease (harmful to student or others)	
Specific behavior to increase (helps student meet an important need)	

Problems you are experiencing as a teacher	Problems you are observing in the class	Problems that affect the students' learning and wellbeing

How would the student describe the problem?

How do these situations tend to start, and what makes them worse?

When is it least likely to happen?	When do things start to "go downhill"?	What changes in body language do you notice?	What does the student say?	What is the peak of the situation?

What would we like to see more of?

What would we like to see less of?

What do we know about the "why" of this behavior?

- What need is the student trying to meet?
- What might the student be moving toward?
- What might the student be moving away from?

Can we offer this student a better way to meet their needs?

Can we alter the set-up to make it easier for the student to succeed?

If we could choose just one thing, what would we prioritize?

4.2 PROACTIVE STRATEGIES

Proactive strategies (green) to use	Opportunities and specific ideas
Teach new skills	
Set up student for success	
Give student access to valued experiences	
Give encouragement and positive feedback	
Manage possible triggers	
Simplify some difficult tasks	
Support during transitions	
Preview and prepare	

4.3 RESPONSIVE STRATEGIES

Responsive strategies (yellow) to use	
Reacting to early signs of difficulty	
Help for student to refocus	
Opportunities for self-regulation	

Recovery strategies (red) to use	
Coping in crisis	
Prioritizing safety	
De-escalating	

4.4 STEP-BY-STEP PLAN

Duration	Specific strategies	Student will be able to...
High support for . . . . . days		
Medium support for . . . . . days		
Lower support for . . . . . days		

4.5 PLANS FOR BEHAVIOR TRACKING

Dates for planned measurement and observation:			

What behavior are we tracking?
(Be as clear and specific as possible)

Who will measure (name of student or staff)?	

How will we measure?
- Instances per hour (rate)
- Total time (e.g., seconds or minutes)
- Total instances per day
- Yes/No (per interval)

How will we summarize?
- Graph
- Chart

References

Ackerlund Brandt, J. A., Dozier, C. L., Juanico, J. F., Laudont, C. L., & Mick, B. R. (2015). The value of choice as a reinforcer for typically developing children. *Journal of Applied Behavior Analysis, 48*(2), 344–362.

Armstrong, D. (2018). Addressing the wicked problem of behaviour in schools. *International Journal of Inclusive Education, 22*(9), 997–1013.

Assor, A., Kaplan, H., & Roth, G. (2002). Choice is good but relevance is excellent: Autonomy affecting teacher behaviors that predict students' engagement in learning. *British Journal of Educational Psychology, 72*(2), 261–278.

Ayllon, T., & Michael, J. (1959). The psychiatric nurse as a behavioral engineer 1. *Journal of the Experimental Analysis of Behavior, 2*(4), 323–334.

Barbosa, M., Beeghly, M., Moreira, J., Tronick, E., & Fuertes, M. (2021). Emerging patterns of infant regulatory behavior in the Still-Face Paradigm at 3 and 9 months predict mother–infant attachment at 12 months. *Attachment & Human Development, 23*(6), 814–830.

Barkley, R. A. (2006). Associated cognitive, developmental, and health problems. In R. A. Barkley (ed.) *Attention-Deficit Hyperactivity Disorder: A Handbook for Diagnosis and Treatment* (3rd edn) (pp. 122–183). Guilford Press.

Barkley, R. A., & Cunningham, C. E. (1979). The effects of methylphenidate on the mother–child interactions of hyperactive children. *Archives of General Psychiatry, 36*(2), 201–208.

Booker, J. A., Capriola-Hall, N. N., Greene, R. W., & Ollendick, T. H. (2019). The parent–child relationship and posttreatment child outcomes across two treatments for oppositional defiant disorder. *Journal of Clinical Child & Adolescent Psychology, 49*(3), 405–419.

Bowlby, J. (1979). The Bowlby–Ainsworth attachment theory. *Behavioral and Brain Sciences, 2*(4), 637–638.

Cabello, B., & Terrell, R. (1994). Making students feel like family: How teachers create warm and caring classroom climates. *Journal of Classroom Interaction,* 17–23.

Carter, M., & Driscoll, C. (2007). A conceptual examination of setting events. *Educational Psychology, 27*(5), 655–673.

Catania, A. C., Shimoff, E., & Matthews, B. A. (1989). An experimental analysis of rule-governed behavior. In S. C. Hayes (ed.) *Rule-Governed Behavior* (pp.119–150). Springer.

Cavanagh, M., Quinn, D., Duncan, D., Graham, T., & Balbuena, L. (2017). Oppositional defiant disorder is better conceptualized as a disorder of emotional regulation. *Journal of Attention Disorders, 21*(5), 381–389.

Cirillo, F. (2006). The pomodoro technique (the pomodoro). *Agile Processes in Software Engineering and Extreme Programming, 54*(2), 35.

Coyne, L. W., & Cairns, D. (2016). A relational frame theory analysis of coercive family process. In T. J. Dishion & J. Snyder (eds) *The Oxford Handbook of Coercive Relationship Dynamics* (pp.86–100). Oxford University Press.

Cristofani, C., Sesso, G., Cristofani, P., Fantozzi, P., Inguaggiato, E., Muratori, P., ... & Milone, A. (2020). The role of executive functions in the development of empathy and its association with externalizing behaviors in children with neurodevelopmental disorders and other psychiatric comorbidities. *Brain Sciences, 10*(8), 489.

Deci, E. L., & Ryan, R. M. (eds) (2004). *Handbook of Self-Determination Research.* University of Rochester Press.

Deci, E. L., Koestner, R., & Ryan, R. M. (1999). A meta-analytic review of experiments examining the effects of extrinsic rewards on intrinsic motivation. *Psychological Bulletin, 125*(6), 627.

Delahooke, M. (2020). *Beyond Behaviours: Using Brain Science and Compassion to Understand and Solve Children's Behavioural Challenges.* Hachette UK.

Dickson, K. S., Ciesla, J. A., & Zelic, K. (2017). The role of executive functioning in adolescent rumination and depression. *Cognitive Therapy and Research, 41*(1), 62–72.

Dodge, K. A., & Pettit, G. S. (2003). A biopsychosocial model of the development of chronic conduct problems in adolescence. *Developmental Psychology, 39*(2), 349.

Drabick, D. A., Bubier, J., Chen, D., Price, J., & Lanza, H. I. (2011). Source-specific oppositional defiant disorder among inner-city children: Prospective prediction and moderation. *Journal of Clinical Child & Adolescent Psychology, 40*(1), 23–35.

Durand, V. M. (2011). *Optimistic Parenting: Hope and Help for You and Your Challenging Child*. Paul H. Brookes.

Dutton Tillery, A., Varjas, K., Meyers, J., & Collins, A. S. (2010). General education teachers' perceptions of behavior management and intervention strategies. *Journal of Positive Behavior Interventions, 12*(2), 86–102.

Dweck, C. S. (2008). Mindsets: How praise is harming youth and what can be done about it. *School Library Media Activities Monthly, 24*(5), 55.

Eisenberger, N. I., Lieberman, M. D., & Williams, K. D. (2003). Does rejection hurt? An fMRI study of social exclusion. *Science, 302*(5643), 290–292.

Elbla, A. I. F. (2012). Is punishment (corporal or verbal) an effective means of discipline in schools? Case study of two basic schools in Greater Khartoum/Sudan. *Procedia – Social and Behavioral Sciences, 69*, 1656–1663.

Fabelo, T., Thompson, M. D., Plotkin, M., Carmichael, D., Marchbanks, M. P., & Booth, E. A. (2011). *Breaking Schools' Rules: A Statewide Study of How School Discipline Relates to Students' Success and Juvenile Justice Involvement*. Council of State Governments Justice Center, New York.

Ferguson, P. (2011). Student perceptions of quality feedback in teacher education. *Assessment & Evaluation in Higher Education, 36*(1), 51–62.

Fergusson, D. M., & Horwood, L. J. (1998). Exposure to interparental violence in childhood and psychosocial adjustment in young adulthood. *Child Abuse & Neglect, 22*(5), 339–357.

Garwood, J. D., Vernon-Feagans, L., & Family Life Project Key Investigators. (2017). Classroom management affects literacy development of students with emotional and behavioral disorders. *Exceptional Children, 83*(2), 123–142.

Geer, J. H., Davison, G. C., & Gatchel, R. I. (1970). Reduction of stress in humans through nonveridical perceived control of aversive stimulation. *Journal of Personality and Social Psychology, 16*(4), 731.

Gopalan, M., & Nelson, A. A. (2019). Understanding the racial discipline gap in schools. *AERA Open, 5*(2), 2332858419844613.

Gottman, J. M. (2011). *The Science of Trust: Emotional Attunement for Couples*. W.W. Norton & Company.

Greene, R. W. (1998). *The Explosive Child: A New Approach for Understanding and Parenting Easily Frustrated, Chronically Inflexible Children*. HarperCollins Publishers.

Greene, R. W. (2008). *Lost at School: Why Our Kids with Behavioral Challenges Are Falling Through the Cracks and How We Can Help Them*. Scribner.

Greene, R. W. (2018). How to teach the most challenging youth to problem solve and reduce staff injuries. *Juvenile Justice*, January 31. Available at: https://jjie.org/2018/01/31/how-to-teach-the-most-challenging-youth-to-problem-solve-and-reduce-staff-injuries-recidivism.

Greene, R. W., & Ablon, J. S. (2005). *Treating Explosive Kids: The Collaborative Problem-Solving Approach*. Guilford Press.

Gregory, A., & Weinstein, R. S. (2008). The discipline gap and African Americans: Defiance or cooperation in the high school classroom. *Journal of School Psychology, 46*(4), 455–475.

Gregory, A., Skiba, R. J., & Mediratta, K. (2017). Eliminating disparities in school discipline: A framework for intervention. *Review of Research in Education, 41*(1), 253–278.

Griffin, M. G., Goodman, B. F., Chesher, R. E., & Kecala, N. M. (2020). Psychophysiology of traumatic stress and posttraumatic stress disorder. In R. H. Paul, L. E. Salminen, J. Heaps, & L. M. Cohen (eds) *The Wiley Encyclopedia of Health Psychology* (pp.287–292). Wiley.

Guinther, P. M., & Dougher, M. J. (2015). The clinical relevance of stimulus equivalence and relational frame theory in influencing the behavior of verbally competent adults. *Current Opinion in Psychology, 2*, 21–25.

Hamre, B. K., & Pianta, R. C. (2005). Can instructional and emotional support in the first-grade classroom make a difference for children at risk of school failure? *Child Development, 76*(5), 949–967.

Hanley, G. P., Jin, C. S., Vanselow, N. R., & Hanratty, L. A. (2014). Producing meaningful improvements in problem behavior of children with autism via synthesized analyses and treatments. *Journal of Applied Behavior Analysis, 47*(1), 16–36.

Harris, R., Tobias, M., Jeffreys, M., Waldegrave, K., Karlsen, S., & Nazroo, J. (2006). Racism and health: The relationship between experience of racial discrimination and health in New Zealand. *Social Science & Medicine, 63*(6), 1428–1441.

Iwata, B. A., Dorsey, M. F., Slifer, K. J., Bauman, K. E., & Richman, G. S. (1982). Toward a functional analysis of self-injury. *Analysis and Intervention in Developmental Disabilities, 2*(1), 3–20.

Jones, R. M., Somerville, L. H., Li, J., Ruberry, E. J., Libby, V., Glover, G., & Casey, B. J. (2011). Behavioral and neural properties of social reinforcement learning. *Journal of Neuroscience, 31*(37), 13039–13045.

Jussim, L., & Harber, K. D. (2005). Teacher expectations and self-fulfilling prophecies: Knowns and unknowns, resolved and unresolved controversies. *Personality and Social Psychology Review, 9*(2), 131–155.

Kern, L., Vorndran, C. M., Hilt, A., Ringdahl, J. E., Adelman, B. E., & Dunlap, G. (1998). Choice as an intervention to improve behavior: A review of the literature. *Journal of Behavioral Education, 8*(2), 151–169.

Kern, L., Mantegna, M. E., Vorndran, C. M., Bailin, D., & Hilt, A. (2001). Choice of task sequence to reduce problem behaviors. *Journal of Positive Behavior Interventions, 3*(1), 3–10.

Kleine Deters, R., Naaijen, J., Rosa, M., Aggensteiner, P. M., Banaschewski, T., Saam, M. C., ... & Dietrich, A. (2020). Executive functioning and emotion recognition in youth with oppositional defiant disorder and/or conduct disorder. *World Journal of Biological Psychiatry*, *21*(7), 539–551.

Logan, F. A., & Spanier, D. (1970). Chaining and nonchaining delay of reinforcement. *Journal of Comparative and Physiological Psychology*, *72*(1), 98.

Matheson, A. S., & Shriver, M. D. (2005). Training teachers to give effective commands: Effects on student compliance and academic behaviors. *School Psychology Review*, *34*(2), 202–219.

Mazur, J. E. (1991). Choice with probabilistic reinforcement: Effects of delay and conditioned reinforcers. *Journal of the Experimental Analysis of Behavior*, *55*(1), 63–77.

McPartland, B. (2015, June 3). French schools move to ban 'teeth-sucking.' *The Local*. Available at: www.thelocal.fr/20150603/french-schools-move-to-ban-teeth-sucking

Miles, S. B., & Stipek, D. (2006). Contemporaneous and longitudinal associations between social behavior and literacy achievement in a sample of low-income elementary school children. *Child Development*, *77*(1), 103–117.

Minahan, J., & Rappaport, N. (2012). *The Behavior Code: A Practical Guide to Understanding and Teaching the Most Challenging Students*. Harvard Education Press.

Mischel, W., & Ebbesen, E. B. (1970). Attention in delay of gratification. *Journal of Personality and Social Psychology*, *16*(2), 329.

Mitchell, G. (2018). An implicit bias primer. *Virginia Journal of Social Policy & the Law*, *25*, 27.

Morris, S. S., Musser, E. D., Tenenbaum, R. B., Ward, A. R., Martinez, J., Raiker, J. S., ... & Riopelle, C. (2020). Emotion regulation via the autonomic nervous system in children with attention-deficit/hyperactivity disorder (ADHD): Replication and extension. *Journal of Abnormal Child Psychology*, *48*(3), 361–373.

Murphy, L. K. (2020). *The Declarative Language Handbook: Using a Thoughtful Language Style to Help Kids with Social Learning Challenges Feel Competent, Connected, and Understood*. Self-published.

Murray, D. W., Lawrence, J. R., & LaForett, D. R. (2018). The Incredible Years® Programs for ADHD in young children: A critical review of the evidence. *Journal of Emotional and Behavioral Disorders*, *26*(4), 195–208.

Nock, M. K., Kazdin, A. E., Hiripi, E., & Kessler, R. C. (2007). Lifetime prevalence, correlates, and persistence of oppositional defiant disorder: Results from the National Comorbidity Survey Replication. *Journal of Child Psychology and Psychiatry*, *48*(7), 703–713.

Noordermeer, S. D., Luman, M., Weeda, W. D., Buitelaar, J. K., Richards, J. S., Hartman, C. A., ... & Oosterlaan, J. (2017). Risk factors for comorbid oppositional defiant disorder in attention-deficit/hyperactivity disorder. *European Child & Adolescent Psychiatry*, *26*(10), 1155–1164.

Nowak, C., & Heinrichs, N. (2008). A comprehensive meta-analysis of Triple-P Positive Parenting Program using hierarchical linear modeling: Effectiveness and moderating variables. *Clinical Child and Family Psychology Review*, *11*(3), 114–144.

Nowicki, J. M. (2018). *K-12 Education: Discipline Disparities for Black Students, Boys, and Students with Disabilities*. Report to Congressional Requesters. GAO-18-258. US Government Accountability Office. Available at www.gao.gov/assets/gao-18-258.pdf

Pardini, D. A., & Fite, P. J. (2010). Symptoms of conduct disorder, oppositional defiant disorder, attention-deficit/hyperactivity disorder, and callous-unemotional traits as unique predictors of psychosocial maladjustment in boys: Advancing an evidence base for DSM-V. *Journal of the American Academy of Child & Adolescent Psychiatry*, *49*(11), 1134–1144.

Piazza, C. C., Contrucci, S. A., Hanley, G. P., & Fisher, W. W. (1997). Nondirective prompting and noncontingent reinforcement in the treatment of destructive behavior during hygiene routines. *Journal of Applied Behavior Analysis*, *30*(4), 705–708.

Porges, S. W. (1992). Vagal tone: A physiologic marker of stress vulnerability. *Pediatrics*, *90*(3, Pt 2), 498–504.

Porges, S. W. (2005). The role of social engagement in attachment and bonding. *Attachment and Bonding*, *3*, 33–54.

Porges, S. W. (2009). The polyvagal theory: New insights into adaptive reactions of the autonomic nervous system. *Cleveland Clinic Journal of Medicine*, *76*(Suppl. 2), S86.

Porges, S. W. (2011). *The Polyvagal Theory: Neurophysiological Foundations of Emotions, Attachment, Communication, and Self-Regulation* (Norton Series on Interpersonal Neurobiology). W.W. Norton & Company.

Quinn, M. J., Miltenberger, R. G., & Fogel, V. A. (2015). Using TAGteach to improve the proficiency of dance movements. *Journal of Applied Behavior Analysis*, *48*(1), 11–24.

Reber, D. (2019). *Differently Wired: A Parent's Guide to Raising an Atypical Child with Confidence and Hope*. Workman Publishing.

Reeve, J. (2016). Autonomy-supportive teaching: What it is, how to do it. In W. C. Liu, J. C. K. Wang, & R. R. Ryan (eds) *Building Autonomous Learners* (pp.129–152). Springer.

Reeve, J., & Tseng, C. M. (2011). Cortisol reactivity to a teacher's motivating style: The biology of being controlled versus supporting autonomy. *Motivation and Emotion*, *35*, 63–74.

Reeve, J., Jang, H., Carrell, D., Jeon, S., & Barch, J. (2004). Enhancing students' engagement by increasing teachers' autonomy support. *Motivation and Emotion*, *28*(2), 147–169.

Reilly, E. D., Ritzert, T. R., Scoglio, A. A., Mote, J., Fukuda, S. D., Ahern, M. E., & Kelly, M. M. (2019). A systematic review of values measures in acceptance and commitment therapy research. *Journal of Contextual Behavioral Science*, *12*, 290–304.

Reynolds, S., Lane, S. J., & Thacker, L. (2012). Sensory processing, physiological stress, and sleep behaviors in children with and without autism spectrum disorders. *OTJR: Occupation, Participation and Health*, *32*(1), 246–257.

Ross, K. (2017). *School-Based Interventions for School-Aged Children with Oppositional Defiant Disorder: A Systematic Review*. Master of Social Work Clinical Research Papers. 788. Available at: http://sophia.stkate.edu/msw_papers/788

Ryan, R. M., & Grolnick, W. S. (1986). Origins and pawns in the classroom: Self-report and projective assessments of individual differences in children's perceptions. *Journal of Personality and Social Psychology*, *50*(3), 550.

Ryan, A. M., Gheen, M. H., & Midgley, C. (1998). Why do some students avoid asking for help? An examination of the interplay among students' academic efficacy, teachers' social–emotional role, and the classroom goal structure. *Journal of Educational Psychology*, *90*(3), 528.

Sandberg, D. E., & Yager, T. J. (1991). The Child Behavior Checklist nonclinical standardization samples: Should they be utilized as norms? *Journal of the American Academy of Child & Adolescent Psychiatry*, *30*(1), 124–134.

Sayal, K., Prasad, V., Daley, D., Ford, T., & Coghill, D. (2018). ADHD in children and young people: Prevalence, care pathways, and service provision. *The Lancet Psychiatry*, *5*(2), 175–186.

Schoorl, J., van Rijn, S., de Wied, M., van Goozen, S., & Swaab, H. (2018). Boys with oppositional defiant disorder/conduct disorder show impaired adaptation during stress: An executive functioning study. *Child Psychiatry & Human Development*, *49*(2), 298–307.

Seligman, M. E. P. (1999). Speech at Lincoln Summit [Transcript]. Closing address at the First Positive Psychology Summit held at the Gallup International Research and Education Center in Lincoln, NE, September 9–12. Positive Psychology Center Conference Archives, University of Pennsylvania, Philadelphia, PA.

Seligman, M. E. P. (2006). *Learned Optimism: How to Change Your Mind and Your Life*. Vintage.

Serwatka, T. S., Deering, S., & Grant, P. (1995). Disproportionate representation of African Americans in emotionally handicapped classes. *Journal of Black Studies*, *25*(4), 492–506.

Shalev, R. S., & Gross-Tsur, V. (2001). Developmental dyscalculia. *Pediatric Neurology*, *24*(5), 337–342. Available at: http://centro-migo.com/wp-content/uploads/2015/04/Developmental-dyscalculia-2001.pdf

Siegel, D. J., & Bryson, T. P. (2012). *The Whole-Brain Child*. Random House.

Sinha, P., Kjelgaard, M. M., Gandhi, T. K., Tsourides, K., Cardinaux, A. L., Pantazis, D., ... & Held, R. M. (2014). Autism as a disorder of prediction. *Proceedings of the National Academy of Sciences*, *111*(42), 15220–15225.

Skinner, B. F. (1974). *About Behaviorism*. Knopf.

Skinner, B. F. (1957). The experimental analysis of behavior. *American Scientist*, *45*(4), 343–371.

Skinner, B. F. (1981). The shaping of a behaviorist: Part Two of an autobiography. *Behaviorism*, *9*(1), 95–97.

Skinner, B. F. (1984). The evolution of behavior. *Journal of the Experimental Analysis of Behavior*, *41*(2), 217.

Skowron, E. A., Cipriano-Essel, E., Benjamin, L. S., Pincus, A. L., & van Ryzin, M. J. (2013). Cardiac vagal tone and quality of parenting show concurrent and time-ordered associations that diverge in abusive, neglectful, and non-maltreating mothers. *Couple and Family Psychology: Research and Practice*, *2*(2), 95.

Thomson, N. D., & Centifanti, L. C. (2018). Proactive and reactive aggression subgroups in typically developing children: The role of executive functioning, psychophysiology, and psychopathy. *Child Psychiatry & Human Development*, *49*(2), 197–208.

van de Pol, J., Volman, M., & Beishuizen, J. (2010). Scaffolding in teacher–student interaction: A decade of research. *Educational Psychology Review*, *22*(3), 271–296.

Walker, P. (2009). The 4Fs: A trauma typology in complex PTSD. Available at: www.pete-walker.com/fourFs_TraumaTypologyComplexPTSD

White, K. J., Sherman, M. D., & Jones, K. (1996). Children's perceptions of behavior problem peers: Effects of teacher feedback and peer-reputed status. *Journal of School Psychology*, *34*(1), 53–72.

Williams, J. (2018). *"It Just Grinds You Down:" Persistent Disruptive Behaviour in Schools and What Can Be Done About It*. Policy Exchange.

Wymbs, B. T., Pelham W. E., Jr, Molina, B. S., Gnagy, E. M., Wilson, T. K., & Greenhouse, J. B. (2008). Rate and predictors of divorce among parents of youths with ADHD. *Journal of Consulting and Clinical Psychology*, *76*(5), 735.

Resources

Here are some of the resources that have inspired "lightbulb moments" for me, helping me see my students, clients, and even my own children in a new way. In many cases, I read these resources and thought: "I wish someone had told me this years ago!" As a professional, I have sometimes spent too much time with my own clinical clan, and not enough time eavesdropping on important conversations that were happening in other disciplines. I want to share these titles with you as a starting point, knowing that there are wonderful new books published every year. Remember, best practices will continue to change as scientific research emerges and cultural norms shift, and I hope you will continue to glean new knowledge and find gems to add to your ever-growing library.

Lost at School: Why Our Kids with Behavioral Challenges are Falling Through the Cracks and How We Can Help Them by Ross W. Greene

If you feel as if you have been alone in your classroom, trying to mind-read your students or pre-empt their difficult behaviour, this book can open up some refreshing new opportunities for you. Dr Greene lays out a framework for setting up constructive conversations with your students that can (a) help you understand the problem from your students' perspective and (b) invite your student to problem-solve with you.

Beyond Behaviors: Using Brain Science and Compassion to Understand and Solve Children's Behavioral Challenges by Mona Delahooke

This book came into my life at just the right time. I was stressed and frustrated because I was looking at every new behaviour struggle as a challenge to my competence as a parent. I could see that I was getting trapped in power struggles, and I needed a new perspective. Dr Delahooke's work helped me to respond to aggressive and ugly behaviours in a more compassionate way, and to be more cognizant of my own emotional ups and downs.

The Behavior Code: A Practical Guide to Understanding and Teaching the Most Challenging Students by Jessica Minahan and Nancy Rappaport

I came across this book quite recently, and I was stunned at the way the authors tackle complex behavioral issues with clarity and accessible insights. Instead of offering a one-size-fits-all solution or a recipe book for gaining compliance, the authors keep the focus on the student, to help you understand their behaviour as it connects to each individual context.

Declarative Language Handbook: Using a Thoughtful Language Style to Help Kids with Social Learning Challenges Feel Competent, Connected, and Understood by Linda K. Murphy

I'm so glad a colleague recommended this book to me, because it gives so many powerful examples of how to communicate without giving commands. The author makes a strong case for how declarative language is not only a respectful way to give information, but also an opportunity for teaching inference, social skills, and problem-solving.

How to Talk When Kids Won't Listen: Whining, Fighting, Meltdowns, Defiance, and Other Challenges of Childhood (The How To Talk Series) by Joanna Faber and Julie King

This book is quite new, but its title might sound familiar to you. In fact, the authors of this book were raised by the authors of the classic book *How to Talk so Kids Will Listen, and Listen so Kids Will Talk* (Faber and Mazlish), and they have compiled this book (with the help of first-hand experience) to help exasperated adults with the most commonly-asked questions. The advice within is excellent for staying creative and flexible in difficult moments.

The Whole-Brain Child: 12 Revolutionary Strategies to Nurture Your Child's Developing Mind by Daniel J. Siegel and Tina Payne Bryson

Students come into your classroom with big, roiling emotions, and a developing set of coping skills. Some of your interactions will be based in logic and reason, while others will be quite raw. If you are looking to develop a more sensitive and supportive approach to children who get carried away with their feelings, this book offers practical examples and a compassionate approach. I still think of this book when I'm parenting, because it built up my confidence and helped me to stick with a gentle and thoughtful approach, even when I'm tempted to use control-based tactics.

Subject Index

Author Index